Transforming Your
RELATIONSHIPS

AN ACTION PLAN FOR LOVE THAT LASTS

THOMAS NELSON PUBLISHERS®

Nashville

Transforming Your RELATIONSHIPS

AN ACTION PLAN FOR LOVE THAT LASTS

DR. RONN ELMORE

THOMAS NELSON PUBLISHERS®

Nashville

Published by Thomas Nelson, Inc.
P.O. Box 141000
Nashville, TN 37214

ISBN: 0-7852-5071-9

Printed in the United States of America

03 04 05 06 07- 5 4 3 2 1

Foreword

Perhaps you've heard the saying "It's lonely at the top." For some people, that maxim is true, and often the more time you spend in the spotlight, the lonelier life can be. But I have great news for you today: *It doesn't have to be that way.* In fact, I believe your life as a leading lady can be filled with good friendships, strong family relationships, and dependable, high-quality professional associations. Unless you truly are a person God has chosen to be single, I also believe you can share your life fully with a man and enjoy the healthy intimacy God desires the two of you to experience in marriage.

I am delighted that Dr. Ronn Elmore has taken the time to share his phenomenal insights into relationships in this workbook. Dr. Elmore is one of America's foremost experts on love, marriage, family, and relationships, and is often called "The Relationship Doctor." He is a husband, a father, a minister and a relationship therapist known for his challenging and spiritual approach to unconditional commitment in marriage. In addition, he is the author of *How to Love a Black Man, How to Love a Black Woman,* and *An Outrageous Commitment: The 48 Vows of an Indestructible Marriage.* I really believe he can help you enhance your interpersonal skills and enable you to enjoy positive change in your relationships from now on.

In order to help you get started on your journey towards transformed relationships, I'd like to take a moment to walk you through each of the features you will find in the pages of this workbook so that you will understand why we have included them and what I hope your interaction with them will accomplish in your life.

Introducing: The word speaks for itself. Introductions to each chapter will simply show you the big picture of the subject covered and give you a glimpse of where we are headed in that chapter.

The Main Event: I am delighted by the wealth of sound, practical advice, and godly wisdom in this workbook. This helpful information is presented to you in sections entitled "The Main Event," which is divided into "Acts," just as a stage play is divided into acts. Each act focuses specifically on a particular aspect of the larger subject of the chapter.

You're On: One of my hopes for you as you work through this book is that you will find all kinds of ways to apply its information to your own life. To help you in that purpose, we have included some questions for you to answer. I hope you'll think about them, answer them, and even use an extra sheet of paper or your journal if you find yourself wanting to consider them more thoroughly or respond to them more extensively.

Learn Your Lines: You probably know that God's Word is "living and active," as we read in the Book of Hebrews, but I want you to continue to experience its transforming power in your daily life. Therefore at the end of many acts, you will find several scriptures relating to the subject you have just studied. As the Word gets worked into your mind, it gets worked out in your life, so I believe these scriptures really are keys to helping you unlock personal victory and success.

Coming Soon: I love this part of the workbook because it is your opportunity to dream on paper. These beautifully designed pages at the end of each chapter will allow you to write a synopsis of what you have learned throughout that chapter, to summarize how you will put those lessons into practice, and to take time to really think about your life and your hopes, aspirations, and inspirations.

Action!: Goal-setting is so important to successful living, and that is why we have concluded every chapter with space for you to list specific goals pertaining to the topic of that chapter. I encourage you to use that space to set a few measurable, challenging, attainable goals and to give yourself a deadline and a reward for reaching each one. In the back of the workbook, you will find an Appendix in which you can put all your goals together in one list and prioritize them.

Leading Lady, the lights are coming up, and it is time for you to shine. I hope that you will enjoy this workbook and that it will help you enjoy deep, rich, wonderful relationships with the men who surround you as you take your place on life's center stage.

God bless you,
T. D. Jakes

Contents

Introduction

Would you allow your mind to wander for just a moment and travel back through thousands of years to the very beginning of time? I'd like to offer you a peek into the moment just prior to the world's first marriage. Can you envision that with me?

The Lord God has crafted a flawless earth. It is bursting with color and teeming with life. He has divided the light from the darkness that had covered the face of the deep. He has fashioned the land and the seas, caused grass and herbs and fruit trees to spring forth and hung the stars in place. He has filled the water and the sky with fish and birds, and populated the land with living creatures. He has tenderly shaped the crown of His creation—the man, breathed into him the breath of life and given him dominion over every lesser animal. And upon the completion of each masterpiece, God has gazed upon His handiwork and declared that it was good. Indeed, it was *very* good.

There came a time, though, when God observed that something was not good, and He said, "It is not good that man should be alone; I will make him a helper comparable to him" (Genesis 2:18). And so, God caused a deep sleep to fall upon Adam; He removed one of his ribs and from it, made a woman—the perfect antidote to man's aloneness. When Adam awoke, he had a wife and the first marriage in the history of humanity was born.

Fast forward to the twenty-first century. Leave Adam and Eve in the garden and begin to think about your own life. Maybe you are a married woman who has enjoyed years of peace and joy with your husband, or maybe you have struggled and are still struggling in a marriage that leaves much to be desired. Maybe you are widowed or divorced; perhaps you have never married, but hope to someday. Whatever your particular situation, I believe this workbook is in your possession for a purpose, and I believe you want to see your relational skills honed so that your relationships can be transformed.

Leading lady, you are God's express solution for perhaps the only problem that existed in a perfect creation. As you well know, creation is no longer perfect, and life holds many challenges. A marriage relationship between a man and a woman can be the most glorious partnership imaginable, but we need look no further than the staggering divorce statistics in America today to see that many, many marriages fail. I don't want that to happen to you, and that's why I've put together this workbook.

Whether your primary dealings with men take place in a work environment, within the sacred bond of marriage, or in dating relationships, or social settings, I believe the material in this book will help you understand men better so that you can relate to them more effectively. Building relationship skills can take some time, and I suspect you'll be developing and fine-tuning some of the skills you'll be introduced to here long after you have been through all the chapters and answered all the questions. I can't predict how long it will take for your relationships to be transformed, but I can tell you that you are beginning a journey towards more joy, more blessings, more fun, more intimacy and more life in your marriage than you may have ever thought possible!

The Lady Knows Her Worth

Introducing

As we get started towards our ultimate goal of seeing your relationships transformed, I want to first expose a lie that the enemy has succeeded in getting women to believe for years. Oh, he communicates to different people in different ways, such as "You will finally be worth something when you get married," or, "Everything would be wonderful if I could just get married," or, "All these issues you struggle with now will go away once you get married," or, "I won't feel so rejected and lonely all the time if I get married."

Do any of those lines sound familiar? Has the enemy of your soul ever whispered them—or a similar deception—to you? I need to tell you that they are all lies. Any time you need someone outside of you to fix something inside of you, you are either involved in addiction or idolatry—and neither will go away when a man shows up. A wedding band around a finger does not heal a broken heart; a man in the house will not improve self-esteem; and being a "Mrs." instead of a "Miss" does not eradicate an anger problem, a struggle with feelings of rejection, anxiety, depression or the tendency to be jealous. If you are not yet married, you must believe me: Everything will *not* suddenly be wonderful once you kiss your groom!

No, the truth is that you must be settled and secure in your own worth before you ever share your life with someone else. Otherwise, your troubles will be compounded because the wounds in your heart are likely to attract similar wounds in a man's heart. Then, instead of having one person who is super-sensitive and always feels left out and rejected, we have two! Both are in for a surprise (not the good kind!) when they realize that all of their weakness and all of their wounded places and all of their unresolved hurt are hanging in the air over their new life together. The best relationships are based on God-ordained desire, not on human neediness. When you pursue a relationship with a man, do so because you want him, not because you need him. Be in relationship out of your wholeness, not out of your woundedness.

This is why I must write to you about your self-esteem before we delve into anything else. (Even if you are already married and have been for years, you may still struggle with aspects of your identity and self-worth, so don't skip this chapter!) You must have a strong, healthy relationship with God and with yourself before you can have a positive relationship with anybody else. So let's begin to work through this matter of self-worth and make sure that you become the highly valued, confident, whole woman that God intends for you to be.

There is only one source in which you can find out the truth about yourself, and it is in God alone.

The Main Event

Act 1: What Does God Think About You?

There is only one source in which you can find out the truth about yourself, and it is in God alone. Other people will not always tell you the truth; accolades and accomplishments may bring momentary applause, but these achievements don't speak to your soul; and your feelings—good heavens, your feelings are the most fickle of all! So who can you trust to tell you the truth about yourself? Only God. And the best place to discover what He thinks about you is in His Word.

I could write pages and pages trying to persuade you that God loves you, that He accepts you completely, that He sings and dances because He thinks you are so terrific, and that He wanted you so much that He sacrificed the only Son He had. But no matter how hard I tried to convince you, those words would still be mine. They would still be words of human origin. So I want to give you a list of God's words about you; those are the only words that are living and active; those are the only words that have the power to bring change. Scripture is loaded with God's thoughts about you, so feel free to explore your Bible and find others that are not listed here. For now, take a look at just some of what He says to you:

I want to give you a list of God's words about you; those are the only words that are living and active; those are the only words that have the power to bring change.

◆ You are loved with an everlasting love, and the Lord draws you to Himself with loving-kindness (Jeremiah 31:3).

◆ You are forgiven and redeemed through the blood of Jesus (Ephesians 1:7).

◆ You were chosen in Christ before the foundation of the world, that you should be holy and blameless before Him in love (Ephesians 1:4).

◆ You are accepted and brought near to God (Ephesians 1:6; 2:13).

◆ You are more than a conqueror through Christ, who loves you (Romans 8:37).

◆ You are the head and not the tail; you are above only and not beneath (Deuteronomy 28:13).

◆ You always triumph in Christ Jesus (2 Corinthians 2:14).

◆ You are the righteousness of God in Christ (2 Corinthians 5:21).

◆ You are complete in Christ (Colossians 2:10).

◆ You can do all things through Christ who strengthens you (Philippians 4:13).

You're On

1. Do you ever struggle to believe God loves you? Why? How can you win that battle? (Even if you need to schedule therapy sessions with a minister or godly counselor, do so. Your security in God is worth it!)

_____

_____

_____

_____

_____

_____

_____

_____

_____

_____

_____

_____

_____

_____

Do your thoughts about yourself agree with God's?

2. I'd like for you to choose one of the scriptures on pages 3 and 4 that most deeply touched you and write it down, memorize it, meditate on it, and knead it into your heart until you are absolutely convinced that it is true *about you.* Which one will you choose? (The verses are different from the ones in "Learn Your Lines." I hope you will memorize and meditate on those as well).

3. Look now at "Learn Your Lines" on page 8 and re-write one of them in the space below, making it personal. For instance, "God's thoughts towards me, (your name), are full of peace. They are not evil. He wants to give me a future and a hope."

_____

_____

_____

_____

_____

_____

_____

_____

_____

_____

_____

_____

_____

_____

_____

If you want to find out how you really feel about yourself, listen to what you say.

Learn Your Lines

*For I know the thoughts that I think toward you,
says the Lord, thoughts of peace and not of evil,
to give you a future and a hope.*
Jeremiah 29:11

*There is therefore now no condemnation to those
who are in Christ Jesus, who do not walk according
to the flesh, but according to the Spirit.*
Romans 8:1

*For this reason I bow my knees to the Father, . . . that He
would grant you, according to the riches of His glory, to be
strengthened with might through His Spirit in the inner man,
that Christ may dwell in your hearts through faith; that you,
being rooted and grounded in love, may be able to comprehend
with all the saints what is the width and length and depth and
height—to know the love of Christ which passes knowledge . . .*
Ephesians 3:14-19

Act 2: What Do You Think About Yourself?

Now that you have acquainted yourself with some of God's thoughts about you, let me ask you: do your thoughts about yourself agree with His? Or have the lies of the enemy been so established in your thinking that you believe his negative, deceptive messages about you?

Maybe it has not ever occurred to you to examine your thoughts towards yourself, and if so, may I make a suggestion? Jesus said, in Matthew 12:34, that, "out of the abundance of the heart the mouth speaks." In other words, if you want to find out how you really feel, listen to what you say. Do you make excuses for your failures or mistakes? Do you say things like "I'm just like this. I'll never change." Is there a hint of hopelessness in your voice when you talk about your future? Or, on the other hand, do your words indicate that you are secure in Jesus, convinced that the Lord loves you and confident in His plans for your life?

Proverbs 18:21a tells us "Death and life are in the power of the tongue." That means you can use your words to put certain thoughts to death and to help others take root and grow in your heart and in your belief system. You need the power of God's Word when you are replacing the enemy's lies about yourself with God's truth. Because words are so powerful, I have taken the verses you read in Act 1 and put them in the form of confessions. I believe that speaking the truth of the Word will be extremely helpful as you develop a new way of thinking about your wonderful self!

> *You can use your words to put certain thoughts to death and to help others take root and grow in your heart and in your belief system.*

- ◆ I am loved with an everlasting love, and the Lord draws me to Himself with lovingkindness (Jeremiah 31:3).

- ◆ I am forgiven and redeemed through the blood of Jesus (Ephesians 1:7).

◆ I was chosen in Christ before the foundation of the world, that I should be holy and blameless before Him in love (Ephesians 1:4).

◆ I am accepted and brought near to God (Ephesians 1:6; 2:13).

◆ I am more than a conqueror through Christ, who loves me (Romans 8:37).

◆ I am the head and not the tail; I am above only and not beneath (Deuteronomy 28:13).

◆ I always triumph in Christ Jesus (2 Corinthians 2:14).

◆ I am the righteousness of God in Christ (2 Corinthians 5:21).

◆ I am complete in Christ (Colossians 2:10).

◆ I can do all things through Christ who strengthens me (Philippians 4:13).

You're On

1. What do your words reveal about your self-image?

2. Will you commit to speak well of yourself? Will you stop yourself when you hear negative words coming out of your mouth about your appearance, your abilities, your potential or anything else about yourself? Will you replace that negative with positive confessions? Write those positive confessions here and then say them aloud.

_____

_____

_____

_____

_____

_____

_____

_____

_____

_____

_____

_____

_____

_____

3. Of the confessions listed on page 12, which two or three will you really "own" and memorize and stand on? Why are those two or three most important to you?

_____

_____

_____

_____

_____

_____

_____

_____

_____

_____

_____

_____

_____

_____

_____

_____

_____

_____

_____

_____

Learn Your Lines

The Lord your God in your midst, the Mighty One, will save;
He will rejoice over you with gladness, He will quiet you with
His love, He will rejoice over you with singing.
Zephaniah 3:17

For I am persuaded that neither death nor life,
nor angels nor principalities nor powers, nor things present
nor things to come, nor height nor depth, nor any other created
thing, shall be able to separate us from the love of God
which is in Christ Jesus our Lord.
Romans 8:38, 39

Therefore, if anyone is in Christ, he is a new creation; old
things have passed away; behold, all things have become new.
2 Corinthians 5:17

COMING SOON

*H*ere's your chance to get some things down on paper. Write whatever is in your heart after completing this chapter. If you need some suggestions, think about the following questions and choose one or more to focus on. What will you need to do in order to improve your sense of self-worth? Do you need to forgive someone and let go of the pain or anger that his or her actions have caused you? Do you need to forgive and forget hurtful or untrue words that have been spoken against you in the past? When you think about the woman you can become and the healthy self-concept you can develop, what good do you anticipate? How can better self-esteem serve your relationship with your husband or your husband-to-be?

_____

_____

_____

_____

_____

_____

_____

_____

_____

ACTION!

*B*ased on what you have learned in this chapter, what are three concise, measurable, attainable goals you will set for yourself as you learn to accept God's perception of you and value yourself more and more? You may want to list books you will read, scriptures you will memorize, or specific things you will do to pamper or celebrate yourself. Be sure to include a schedule and target date for reaching each goal and a reward for accomplishing it.

1. Goal: _____

Schedule and target completion date: _____

Reward: _____

_____

2. Goal: _____

Schedule and target completion date: _____

Reward: _____

_____

3. Goal: _____

Schedule and target completion date: _____

Reward: _____

_____

Notes

Notes

2
The Lady Gets Real

Introducing

ost little girls dream of falling in love. They envision a fairy-tale romance, a beautiful wedding, a romantic honeymoon, and a happily-ever-after that would put a princess to shame. A problem arises, though, when starry-eyed little girls carry their dreams into their womanhood. It is one thing for a four-year-old to walk around her living room in her mother's nightgown, with a towel draped over her head pretending to be a princess or a bride, but it is something else altogether for a twenty-four-year-old woman or a thirty-four-year-old woman to walk through her life with her head full of fantasy. *That*, my sister, is dangerous.

I am well aware that women of all races and genders and ages struggle with this issue of fantasy. I often say that the most difficult thing about real life is that it is so real! When it's real, it can be difficult, and for that reason, it's easy to fall prey to fantasy because a woman's life is surrounded by products and materials that breed it—romance novels, soap operas, movies, love songs, shampoo commercials, even the names of perfumes!

It takes a strong woman in today's culture to withstand the temptation to let her mind wander down the romance path.

Leading lady, I believe you are a strong woman. I believe you are capable of such nobility of thought that you can banish fantasy from the kingdom of your mind forever. I believe you are strong enough to live a real life with a real man. And in this chapter, I'd like to help you learn to do that. Even if you do not wrestle with imaginary scenarios or wishes that have become fantasies, I hope you'll read this material, because you may be able to help someone who does.

The Main Event

Act 1: Too Good to Be True

I'm sure you've heard the old saying "If it sounds too good to be true, it probably is!" Perhaps those words have had such staying power in American culture because we have seen them borne out many times, in a multitude of situations. It's not that what is true is never good, but what is true is seldom, if ever, perfect—especially when it comes to your relationship with a man. There is something about perfection in a romantic relationship—being perfectly loved and perfectly understood—that we long for. Sometimes, we long for it because we've never had it; sometimes we long for it because we believe we deserve it. Sometimes, the longing drives us to fantasize about the lives we wish we had.

We are so much more attracted to the glamorous existence we can create in the privacy of

> *It's not that what is true is never good; but what is true is seldom, if ever, perfect—especially when it comes to your relationship with a man.*

our own minds than we are to dirty dishes and dirty socks, to oil changes and mood swings, to having more month than we have money, to deadlines and dying enthusiasm. Let's face it: fantasy is much more fun than real life! And so, in our minds, we begin to imagine ourselves living lives in which our spouse is perfect, our finances are perfect, our behavior is perfect, our sex life is perfect, our children are perfect, our home is perfect, our social life is perfect—anything that would normally challenge us becomes perfect in the safety of the space between our ears.

> *Fantasy is a lethal combination of denial and escape fueled by imagination, and its only antidote is honesty.*

Fantasy is a lethal combination of denial and escape fueled by imagination, and its only antidote is honesty. I need to tell you the truth right now: You are not perfect; your man is not perfect; your relationship will not be perfect. If you can accept the reality of the shortcomings, weaknesses, challenges, insecurities, areas-that-need-improvement, temptations and fears in yourself and in your man, then you can begin to embrace the reality in which you live and that reality can become better than anything you've ever dreamed of.

I hope you understand that I am confronting this matter of fantasy for one reason—and it is not to make you ashamed, and it is not to bring conviction upon you. The transformation of your relationships depends upon your honesty, so I am addressing this with you because I want you to enjoy a pure, deep, intimate, honest relationship with the man in your life. I am asking you to run a reality check on your expectations of your man and your expectations of your relationship with him. I challenge you to see yourself as you are and to see your man as he is; I also challenge you to risk allowing him to see the real you. I want the real you to relate to the real him. I want you to know each other for who you really are, not for who you imagine each other to be. This is the only way you can grow in intimacy and develop a real, healthy, transparent, rich, and vibrant partnership. Fantasy always leads to disappointment, sometimes shattering disappointment, because when you are a real live human being, real life will eventually butt in. And when it does, I want you to be able to greet it with grace and live it with skill and in truth.

> *I challenge you to see yourself as you are and to see your man as he is; I also challenge you to risk allowing him to see the real you.*

You're On

1. In what ways do you need to eliminate fantasy from your thinking and embrace the truth? Here are a few areas to think about: yourself, your man's personality, your man's abilities, your finances and financial capabilities, your sex life, your future.

_____

_____

_____

_____

_____

_____

_____

_____

_____

_____

_____

_____

_____

_____

When you are a real live human being, real life will eventually butt in.

2. How has fantasy robbed you of real life in the past? How can you begin to face real life and accept the things that are less than perfect?

_____

_____

_____

_____

_____

_____

_____

_____

_____

Fables, fantasies, and myths about sex probably created an entire set of false expectations that do not exist anywhere in the realm of reality.

_____

_____

_____

_____

_____

_____

_____

_____

3. Are you willing to take the risks I've challenged you to take—to see the real you, see your real man, and allow him to see you for the woman you really are?

Learn Your Lines

Behold, You desire truth in the inward parts,
and in the hidden part, You will make me to know wisdom.
Psalm 51:6

And you shall know the truth,
and the truth shall make you free.
John 8:32

Finally, brethren, whatever things are true,
whatever things are noble, whatever things are just,
whatever things are pure, whatever things are lovely,
whatever things are of good report, if there is any virtue and
if there is anything praiseworthy—meditate on these things.
Philippians 4:8

Act 2: Sexually Speaking

I know, I know. Books on relationships are not supposed to talk about sex in the second chapter! A person is supposed to have to wade through 100 pages of other material before she gets to this part. Not so in this book. No doubt, you have already figured out that this is no-nonsense workbook designed to challenge you and it is not afraid to tackle intimate issues. For that reason, I want to write frankly to you right now about the area of sexual fantasy.

I don't know how your temptation towards sexual fantasy started. It could have been in conversations with your older sister, or in something you saw on a television or movie screen, or in a traumatic situation over which you had absolutely no control. But somehow, fables, fantasies, and myths about sex made their way into your mind. Once they had occupied a place in your thinking, they convinced you that they were true—which set you up for a gamut of experiences ranging from disappointment, confusion, and frustration to shame and unspeakable pain. They probably created an entire set of false expectations that do not exist anywhere in the realm of reality. Under such circumstances, your sex life is doomed to fail.

In my book, *How to Love a Black Man*, I wrote, "anything that unrealistically exalts or debases some aspect of sexuality is dangerous" (Dr. Ronn Elmore, *How to Love a Black Man* [New York: Warner Books, 1996], 188). It doesn't matter if your man is black, white, red, yellow, brown or green—that statement is still true. That is why your thoughts about sexuality and your approach to your sexual relationship must be based in reality. Only then can you take steps towards a truly intimate love life that is not only charged with passion, but also with purity and truth.

Now, be assured that you are not going to find quality advice in a romance novel. Romance novels are fiction, and by definition, fiction is not true! Similarly, you are not likely to read a godly approach to sexuality in the magazines at the supermarket or to hear it on a talk show. Furthermore, your spouse is not a made-up soap opera actor who has memorized a series of steamy lines. Trust me, you don't want worldly advice; you want straight talk from men and women

> *Your thoughts about sexuality and your approach to your sexual relationship must be based in reality.*

who are grounded in the truth of God's Word. I encourage you to make a commitment to the truth as it pertains to your sexuality and to the physical aspects of your marriage. There are plenty of resources available. I highly recommend these books.

The Five Love Languages
> Dr. Gary Chapman

How to Love a Black Man
> Dr. Ronn Elmore

How to Love a Black Woman
> Dr. Ronn Elmore

An Outrageous Commitment
> Dr. Ronn Elmore

Men Are from Mars, Women Are from Venus
> Dr. John Gray

Your Personality Tree
> Florence Littaur

Seven Secrets About Men Every Woman Should Know
> Dr. Barbara DeAngelis

The Two Sides of Love
> Gary Smalley & Dr. John Trent

Making Peace with Your Partner
> Dr. H. Norman Wright

The Language of Love: How to Quickly Communicate Your Feelings and Needs
> Gary Smalley & Dr. John Trent

Reclaiming Intimacy: Overcoming the Consequences of Premarital Relationships
> Heather Jamison

Keeping Your Family Strong in a World Gone Wrong
> Kevin Leman

*One Home at a Time: Restoring the Soul of America
     Through God's Plan for Your Marriage and Family*
     Dennis Rainey

Other Recommendations:

101 Ways to Date Your Mate
     Debra White Smith
*The Love List: Eight Little Things That Make a
     Big Difference in Your Marriage*
     Drs. Les & Leslie Parrott
Boundaries in Marriage
     Dr. Henry Cloud & Dr. John Townsend
*What Wives Wish Their Husbands Knew
     About Women*
     Dr. James Dobson
Love for a Lifetime
     Dr. James Dobson
Building Your Marriage
     Dennis Rainey
Love is a Decision
     Gary Smalley
Passages of Marriage
     Frank & Mary Alice Minirth, Brian Newman
Love Must Be Tough
     Dr. James Dobson
Personality Plus
     Florence Littaur
Loving Solutions: Overcoming Barriers in Your Marriage
     Dr. Gary Chapman

> *I encourage you to make a commitment to the truth as it pertains to your sexuality and to the physical aspects of your marriage.*

You're On

1. If you struggle with fantasy or myth, how has that affected you negatively? What can you do to overcome those temptations or break those thought patterns?

_____

_____

_____

_____

_____

_____

_____

_____

_____

_____

_____

_____

_____

_____

_____

_____

_____

2. If you are married, have you accepted your sex life for
what it is? If not, will you commit to seek the truth and banish the hurtful deception that comes with fantasy?

_____

_____

_____

_____

_____

_____

_____

_____

_____

_____

_____

_____

_____

_____

_____

_____

_____

_____

_____

_____

3. If you are currently unmarried, but hope to marry someday, what have you learned in this section that will help you
get off to a good start in your physical relationship?

_____

_____

_____

_____

_____

_____

_____

_____

_____

_____

_____

_____

_____

_____

_____

_____

_____

_____

_____

Learn Your Lines

Drink water from your own cistern, and running water from your own well. Should your fountains be dispersed abroad, streams of water in the streets? Let them be your own, and not for strangers with you. Let your fountain be blessed, and rejoice with the wife of your youth. As a loving deer and a graceful doe, let her breasts satisfy you at all times; and always be enraptured with her love.

Proverbs 5:15-19

I charge you, O daughters of Jerusalem,
do not stir up nor awaken love until it pleases.

Song of Solomon 8:4

Marriage is honorable among all, and the bed undefiled; but fornicators and adulterers God will judge.

Hebrews 13:4

COMING SOON

$\mathcal{I}$ suspect that, no matter how fantasy has impacted your life, there is an incredible woman inside of you, and she is well able to live her life completely within the realm of reality. Who is that woman? Who are you, down deep inside? What are your strengths and sources of joy? Would you use the space below to write about the *real* you and your *real* life?

_____

_____

_____

_____

_____

_____

_____

_____

_____

_____

_____

_____

_____

_____

ACTION!

*B*ased on what you have learned in this chapter, what are three concise, measurable, attainable goals you will set for yourself as you learn to have realistic expectations of your dating relationship and/or your marriage? Be sure to include a schedule and target date for reaching each goal and a reward for accomplishing it.

1. Goal: _____

Schedule and target completion date: _____

Reward: _____

_____

2. Goal: _____

Schedule and target completion date: _____

Reward: _____

_____

3. Goal: _____

Schedule and target completion date: _____

Reward: _____

_____

Notes

The Lady Understands Her Man

Introducing

The fruit bowl sits atop the kitchen counter, cradling a colorful arrangement of apples and oranges. The deep reds and bright oranges brighten up an otherwise dull corner, and their brilliant hues seem somehow to dance together in their stillness. If you are in search of a healthy afternoon snack, you've hit the jackpot. But unless you want two pieces of fruit, you will have to choose between an apple and an orange—and the two, through they are both fruits, are vastly different.

The apple's thin skin covers its smooth insides, while the orange's thick peel shrouds its pulpy nourishment. The apple can be a bit bland, compared to the tangy acidity of the orange. The apple is easy to eat—wash it and take a bite. The orange, on the other hand, offers a bit of a challenge in that most people want to peel it before they eat it. Apples bruise easily, while oranges are tough. I could go on, but you can probably see by now that each fruit has its benefits and its drawbacks. Their similarities seem limited to the fact that both are indeed fruits, both grow on trees, and they contain some of the same vitamins. But in taste, texture, and appearance, apples and oranges are as different as—well, apples and oranges.

> *Differences between men and women will lead to one of two things, either frustration or fascination.*

The same is true for men and women—and I'm sure you know that at this point on your journey through life. We are both members of the human race, and we have some of the same physical features—we both have heads and necks and ears and arms and legs and feet. We both have red blood cells and saliva. But when we shift out of the biological and physical realms into mental and emotional territory, it seems all similarities cease. If you are in a relationship with a man and want to see it grow and flourish, you must understand the fundamental differences between men and women. You'll have to learn to live with them and maybe even—dare I say—to celebrate them.

The Main Event

Act 1: Not Better, Not Worse, Just Different

I have observed, over years of relationship counseling, that differences between men and women will lead to one of two things, either frustration or fascination. What determines the outcome? Understanding. When the differences are not understood, they can breed frustration and confusion. When they are understood, they can bring about fascination and celebration.

Chances are, you have already identified many areas in which you and your man are different, but let me list several of them here:

- You and your man think differently.

- You and your man see the world differently.

- You and your man process and communicate emotional issues differently.

- You and your man approach work differently.

- You and your man communicate and express love differently.

- You and your man enjoy and value different things.

- You and your man respond to change differently.

- You and your man handle money differently.

- You and your man deal with conflict differently.

- You and your man are inspired and motivated differently.

The worst possible way to try to understand a man is to filter him through your female grid.

Do you see anything familiar in the list above? I'm sure you do, and I'm sure you could make another list just as long as this one. Being aware of your differences is the first step towards understanding them, so I encourage you to study your man and learn as much as possible about the ways you and he differ. Once you have a grasp on those key differences, try to understand them. Now, let me warn you that the worst possible way to try to understand a man is to filter him through your female grid. Do not try to apply what you understand about yourself or about women to your man. That's akin to trying to learn about apples by examining oranges. You must learn him by knowing *him*, observing *him* and watching *his* responses.

> **One of the biggest obstacles you may face in your pursuit of understanding is the temptation to ask why *the two of you are so vastly different.***

One of the biggest obstacles you may face in your pursuit of understanding is the temptation to ask *why* the two of you are so vastly different. You are different because God created men and women to be different, and to belabor the point of why He did so is to get yourself stuck in a rut, spinning your mental wheels trying to answer the wrong question.

The right question is: *How* do my man and I differ, and *what* can we do to help our differences become a source of delight instead of disappointment? I challenge you to accept the differences that exist between yourself and the man you love; and then not only to accept them, but to embrace them. Like the apples and oranges on the kitchen countertop, your differences can dance.

You're On

1. What do you consider the top three areas of difference between you and your man?

_____

_____

_____

_____

_____

_____

_____

_____

_____

_____

_____

_____

_____

_____

_____

_____

2. How can you learn to accept the differences that exist between yourself and the man you love?

3. In what ways can your differences bring strength to your romantic relationship?

_____

_____

_____

_____

_____

_____

_____

_____

_____

_____

_____

_____

_____

_____

_____

*Like
the apples
and oranges
on the kitchen
countertop, your
differences can
dance.*

Learn Your Lines

But there is a spirit in man, and the breath
of the Almighty gives him understanding.
Job 32:8

He who gets wisdom loves his own soul;
he who keeps understanding will find good.
Proverbs 19:8

If it is possible, as much as depends on you,
live peaceably with all men.
Romans 12:18

Act 2: Dozens of Bridges

As you learn to successfully relate to your man and understand the differences between the two of you, it is critical that you understand that he needs rehearsal time. Of all the differences I could write to you about, this one may prove most helpful. By that, I mean give your man time to process your emotions, think about those important things you need and want from him. Let him mull them over and rehearse them in his brain. After all, he is in a relationship with one of God's leading ladies, and as you step into new-found places of career leadership with additional responsibilities, as you move into levels of ministry you've never before encountered, as you enter into times of new financial prosperity, if your man is able to hold tight to you as God moves you into center stage, it will give him time to adjust to changes and walk in step with you, rather than separately. Don't expect to get from him the immediate answers you may get when you communicate with members of your own sex.

God had a sense of humor when He designed men and women, especially when He got to our heads. Our brains are made up of a right side and a left side. The right side is where we feel emotions and think creatively (*I feel loved when he holds my hand; he must mean this when he says he's tired*. And the left side is for cold, hard facts (*I'm wearing a gray suit; it's a rainy day today*.) Women are naturally born with thousands of bridges, called neurotransmitters, between these two sides of the brain, which allow information or stimuli to quickly cross from one side to the other. For instance, women can say "I love you," cry, and wonder if they left the iron on all in the same sentence. In expressing themselves, most women know what they feel and can speak it instantly.

Men, on the other hand, take longer to process things. Your man will need time to "go underground" and sort through the things that are swirling around inside of him, whether they are his own emotions or feelings you have shared. (Hint: men prefer to do this alone, while women often process feelings with someone else.) A man can quickly understand what he can see, what he can interpret with his senses, what is objective (as opposed to subjective), and what is concrete. It is the nebulous, invisible world of feelings and emotions that he has trouble navigating quickly. He feels—he just doesn't identify his feelings as rapidly as

> *God had a sense of humor when He designed men and women, especially when He got to our heads.*

you do, and it will take him longer to express them. It will also take longer than you think it should for him to understand and process your emotions, so when you dealing in the realm of feelings, patience is indeed a virtue!

For the thousands of neurotransmitters women have, men have dozens. This is comparable to women having high-speed Internet access, while men have the old dial-up method. It has nothing to do with intelligence, but only the speed with which you can switch from one side of the brain to the other. What this means is that men usually take longer to switch from right-brain matters to left-brain issues. They generally do better when dealing with one category of thoughts at a time. So, when you are communicating your feelings, try to stay focused.

> *Give your man time to process your emotions and those important things you need and want from him. Let him mull them over and rehearse them in his brain.*

If you want to talk intimately with your man and see your relationship transformed, it's important to give him time to switch into that mode so he can understand that he's dealing with strictly right-brain matter rather than cold, hard facts. Prepare him for any meaningful conversation by giving him time and warning. By allowing him space and time to process his own feelings and responses, you're more likely to see the deep, inner side of him, with gut-level honesty. In the long run, he'll be encouraged by the success of growing in verbal and emotional intimacy with you.

As you learn to share your feelings with your man and to understand his, here are some points to remember:

◆ He prefers to tackle one issue at a time.

◆ He needs longer than you do, maybe much longer, to understand and process his feelings. Likewise, he needs extra time to process the emotions you express.

◆ He may seem to have "shut down" on you, but he has probably just gone underground to work through his emotions or to process yours.

◆ Don't pressure him to talk; he will talk when he is ready.

◆ The more emotionally charged a situation, the more processing time he will need. Examples of such times include deciding to get married, deciding to buy a house, relocating, changing jobs, grieving over the death of a loved one, etc. He may also need some help, so assist him by asking questions that include choices such as, "Is this fear or is this confusion?" and "Is this anger or is this hurt?"

Men take longer to process their responses to life experiences than women do. Your man will need time to "go underground" and sort through the feelings swirling around inside of him, whether they are his own emotions or feelings you have shared.

You're On

1. How have you imposed your high-speed communication on your man's dial-up method in the past? What have the results been?

_____

_____

_____

_____

_____

_____

_____

_____

For the thousands of neurotransmitters women have, men have dozens.

_____

_____

_____

_____

_____

_____

_____

_____

2. Have you noticed that your man needs more time or space to process certain topics or issues (for example, things dealing with finances or parenting)? What are the subjects that seem to be most difficult or most sensitive or require the most pondering for him? How can you better accommodate him in these situations?

3. What changes do you need to make in your communication-tion style in order to more effectively relate to your man?

_____

_____

_____

_____

_____

_____

_____

Men usually take longer to switch from right-brain matters to left-brain issues. They generally do better when dealing with one category of thoughts at a time.

_____

_____

_____

_____

_____

_____

_____

Learn Your Lines

The heart of him who has understanding seeks knowledge,
but the mouth of fools feeds on foolishness.
Proverbs 15:14

Let your speech always be with grace, seasoned with salt,
that you may know how you ought to answer each one.
Colossians 4:6

Endeavoring to keep the unity of the
Spirit in the bond of peace.
Ephesians 4:3

COMING SOON

*W*hat do you think you can look forward to as you begin to better understand the special man in your life? How can the two of you embrace and celebrate your differences? How do you think increased understanding can improve your relationship? Go ahead and dream a little; use the space below to record what you're hoping for!

_____

_____

_____

_____

_____

_____

_____

_____

_____

_____

_____

_____

_____

_____

_____

_____

ACTION!

*B*ased on what you have learned in this chapter, what are three concise, measurable, attainable goals you will set for yourself as you learn to understand your man, and therefore to relate to him more effectively? Be sure to include a schedule and target date for reaching each goal and a reward for accomplishing it.

1. Goal: _____

Schedule and target completion date: _____

Reward: _____

_____

2. Goal: _____

Schedule and target completion date: _____

Reward: _____

_____

3. Goal: _____

Schedule and target completion date: _____

Reward: _____

_____

Notes

4

The Lady Is Not Ashamed

Introducing

I hope you are not ashamed of the fact that you are a leading lady. For some reason, women sometimes struggle when they are blessed. Sometimes, they are so challenged by success that they work as hard to run from it as they did to reach it. If God has blessed you with success or visibility or influence in finances, ministry, or your career, don't feel like you have to downplay it. Too many women have spent too much time apologizing for the good things God has done in their lives, and I don't want you to be among them. If you're a leading lady, do not be ashamed of it. Don't flaunt your success or define yourself by it; but by all means, don't hide it! A truly transformed relationship requires total transparency and honesty on the part of both the man and the woman, and in order to be honest, you are going to have to let him know that you are indeed a leading lady and to let him see your success. And in order to make the most of your own life, you are going to have to put your best foot forward, exert your best efforts and enjoy their rewards.

The Main Event

Act 1: Be Your Best and Enjoy It

I want to encourage you to be the best you can be everywhere you go, in everything you do, every day of your life. You are a leading lady because you are smart and sophisticated, diligent and determined, poised and professional. You know how to handle yourself, whether you are surrounded by dignitaries or you are serving dinner. But still, there may lurk in you, as there does in so many women, a feeling of unworthiness, a sense that you are losing your balance on your pedestal or a general impression that your success cannot possibly last long because you don't know how to maintain it. Maybe you are one of those women who secretly fears that the man in her life will be jealous or intimidated by her success (We will address this issue specifically in the next chapter). May I remind you that you are a whole woman? Your self-worth is not dependent on anyone else's opinion. So I'd like to help you learn to be your best, no matter who's watching, no matter who wants to hold you back, and no matter what anybody thinks. Leading Lady, you have worked hard to get where you are, and it's time for you to maximize the glorious moment you have and to feel free to fully delight in every blessing that comes your way.

Your blessings may come in various forms, but however they come, they are yours to enjoy. I challenge you to take a look at the areas that follow and ask yourself two questions. First, "Am I being

Be the best you can be everywhere you go, in everything you do, every day of your life.

my best or doing my best in this area of my life?" And second, "Am I enjoying my success in this part of my life and the benefits that accompany it?"

- ◆ Your personal growth and development
- ◆ Your appearance
- ◆ Your career
- ◆ Your finances
- ◆ Your love life
- ◆ Your parenting
- ◆ Your community or volunteer service
- ◆ Your leadership opportunities
- ◆ Your social life
- ◆ Your education

When you are walking in the fullness of your stature as a leading lady and being your best self in every situation, you send an invisible signal to everyone around you that says, "This woman is to be treated well."

You deserve to be treated well—all the time, by everyone. But we all know that it is possible to run into people who do not treat you as they should. When you are walking in the fullness of your stature as a leading lady and being your best self in every situation, you send an invisible signal to everyone around you that says, "This woman is to be treated well." Don't ever let a man mistreat you; a man of quality and character can pick up your signal in a heartbeat. I'll let you in on a secret: the higher your realistic and sincere expectations of him, the more likely he is to deliver on them. When you expect to be treated well and then acknowledge his efforts to treat you well, you can expect this behavior to continue. Be proactive in the way you expect to be treated, because your man will take his cues from you. When you carry yourself well, exude the right mix of confidence and grace, use discretion and behave like the class act of a lady that you are, a man takes notice. He will see the standards he needs to live up to because your attitude will communicate your expectations of him. Let him know that you believe he *can* and *will* treat you with honor, respect, courtesy and dignity—and then watch him do it.

> *When you carry yourself well, exude the right mix of confidence and grace, use discretion and behave like the class act of a lady that you are, a man takes notice.*

You're On

1. Are you being your best in every area of your life? Are you enjoying the benefits of your success? If so, good for you! If not, what areas need improvement? And what changes do you need to make in these areas?

_____

_____

_____

_____

_____

_____

_____

_____

_____

_____

_____

_____

_____

_____

_____

2. Is the man in your life treating you well? If so, do you
acknowledge and appreciate the way he treats you? How do
you acknowledge it? If not, what can you do to let him know
you need to be treated differently?

3. What do your attitudes, behavior, and the way you carry yourself convey about the way you expect to be treated?

_____

_____

_____

_____

_____

_____

_____

_____

_____

Somewhere in his logical mind, every man wants to know there is a part of your life to which he is contributing—and that his contribution is making your life better than it would be if he weren't there.

_____

_____

_____

_____

_____

Learn Your Lines

I know that nothing is better for them than to rejoice, and to do good in their lives, and also that every man should eat and drink and enjoy the good of all his labor — it is the gift of God.
Ecclesiastes 3:12-13

Having then gifts differing according to the grace that is given to us, let us use them:
Romans 12:6a

I, therefore, the prisoner of the Lord, beseech you to walk worthy of the calling with which you were called.
Ephesians 4:1

Act 2: Let Him Contribute

According to scripture, men were created in the mold of Adam, to tend and manage God's creation — to get things done. In general, while women think relationally and emotionally, men think practically, finding ways to go from point A to point B. But somewhere in his logical mind, every man wants to know there is a part of your life to which he is contributing — and that his contribution is making your life better than it would be if he weren't there. Even if you don't need his money, his company, or his words (and you don't), he wants to know that there is some way that he can use his gifts or abilities to invest in your life. He wants to see that although you don't need him, you surely want him. Believe it or not, every man is looking for the opportunity to serve you in ways that elevate your life.

If you are blessed to have a man who is whole and free enough to not be intimidated by your success, he is probably fascinated by you, captivated by your abilities and eager to do all he can to help you get into the spotlight and stay there. He just wants to know that he can be involved in what you are about and to know that there are things he can be for you, do for you, or say to you that no one else on earth can. He needs to hear you say things like this:

- "Nobody makes me laugh like you do!"

- "Nobody encourages me like you do!"

- "Nobody can give a neck rub like you can!"

- "Nobody makes my coffee as perfectly as you do!"

- "Nobody knows what looks good on me like you do!"

- "Nobody motivates me to keep going like you do!"

- "Nobody prays for me like you do!"

- "Nobody makes me feel as safe and secure as you do!"

As I've already encouraged you, do not apologize for your success. But as you ascend the ladder of success, point out the ways that your man steadies the ladder or escorts

> *If you are blessed to have a man who is whole and free enough to not be intimidated by your success, he is probably fascinated by you, captivated by your abilities, and eager to do all he can to help you get into the spotlight and stay there.*

you up to the top of it. There is power in your reminding him of the ways he contributes to your life. Don't leave your man in the audience as a fan while you take center stage. Fans watch and applaud and enjoy the show, but they do not drive the leading lady home. Let your leading man be intimately involved in your life—and be sure to let him know all the ways he makes it possible for you to succeed.

You're On

1. How does your man make your life better?

_____

_____

_____

_____

_____

_____

_____

_____

_____

_____

_____

_____

2. Even though you are a leading lady and you are not needy, how can you let your man know how much you want him?

_____

_____

_____

_____

_____

_____

_____

_____

_____

_____

_____

_____

_____

_____

Don't leave your man in the audience as a fan while you take center stage. Fans watch and applaud and enjoy the show, but they do not drive the leading lady home.

3. What can you do to bring your leading man into the spotlight with you?

Learn Your Lines

*Two are better than one, because they have
a good reward for their labor.*
Ecclesiastes 4:9

Can two walk together, unless they are agreed?
Amos 3:3

Bear one another's burdens, and so fulfill the law of Christ.
Galatians 6:2

COMING SOON

*I*f you have ever withheld your best in any situation or denied yourself the privilege of enjoying your success, I hope this chapter has encouraged you to change. As you look towards the days to come, what do you see when you think of yourself giving the world your very best? What will it be like to enjoy your success, without being afraid of what someone will think? In what ways can your man contribute to your success and share in your rewards?

_____

_____

_____

_____

_____

_____

_____

_____

_____

_____

_____

_____

_____

_____

ACTION!

$\mathcal{B}$ased on what you have learned in this chapter, what are three concise, measurable, attainable goals you will set for yourself in the area of being your best, doing your best, enjoying your success, and allowing your man to make meaningful contributions to your life? Be sure to include a schedule and target date for reaching each goal and a reward for accomplishing it.

1. Goal: _____

Schedule and target completion date: _____

Reward: _____

_____

2. Goal: _____

Schedule and target completion date: _____

Reward: _____

_____

3. Goal: _____

Schedule and target completion date: _____

Reward: _____

_____

Notes

5

The Lady Invites Him to Join Her

Introducing

H e worked the early morning shift at a fast-food restaurant, and spent evenings loading boxes onto eighteen-wheelers in a distribution center. He had little time for sleep and less for recreation. But he didn't mind. After all, he was helping the love of his life pursue her dream. She had convinced him that if he would just help now, while she attended acting school, the day would come when her career would skyrocket and he might not even have to work at all.

He never told her that he wasn't so sure about the stardom she sought. He never told her that he thought he'd prefer his long days of hard work to a red-carpet walk at the Academy Awards. She was so excited that he didn't want to discourage her, so he just kept working to help her finish school.

He was there for every community theatre production and applauded her when no one else did. He was there when she received the call that she'd been chosen as the lead in a denture commercial, and he treated her as though she'd landed a multi-million dollar role in a high-budget movie. But deep inside, he began to fear losing her. He began to wonder if he, the fry chef and the dockworker, would remain attractive to her as she became exposed to people more chic and sophisticated than he. He loved her; he just didn't know that he could hold onto her by helping her fly. And she never told him.

> *Being a leading lady is more than just knowing how to publicly carry yourself while you run a company, a family, or a ministry.*

He began the process of shutting down his heart, but she was too preoccupied with her budding success to notice. She excelled at every part she played and gained the attention of those who had the ability to make her career. Her man was still around, having quit his restaurant job, but he spent most of his time watching television. Passing by his recliner on her way to auditions, she planted a gratuitous kiss on the top of his head and he responded with a grunt. She wished he were more interested in what she was doing. When she finally became a Hollywood hit, he was gone—back to the town where they met. She missed him; he missed her; and he would have looked so nice in a tuxedo.

Oh well, she reasoned, *he wouldn't have enjoyed the premier.*

Oh well, he thought, *she didn't want me anyway.*

The Main Event

Act 1: It Isn't Either/Or

In the previous chapter, I alluded to the fact that some women have a deep fear inside them. It is a fear that takes the form of a question as a woman wonders whether or not her man can handle her if God actually makes her into all He wants her to become—a leading lady who walks into the spotlight of center stage and plays her role with confidence, using all her talents and gifts. With some trepidation, she asks herself, *If I really become successful, will he be able to deal with me and with my life?*

Being a leading lady is more than just knowing how to publicly carry yourself while you run a company, a family, or a ministry. It is more than knowing how to perform brain surgery or bake the world's best lemon pie or design a missile or serve in Congress. It is goes beyond the ability to write a Pulitzer prize-winning book or complete a groundbreaking experience that is nominated for a Nobel. It exceeds graduate degrees and public accolades, limousines and power lunches. Being a leading lady is also the ability to move into the things God has for you without leaving behind the one who loves you.

Some leading ladies will lead at home, some in the ministry, some in a profession. The last thing we want to see is a lady who has career or ministry success, while the one thing that matters most to her goes down the tube. But you see, this is not an either/or matter. It's not a case of *either* having public success, powerful ministry and being placed on center stage as an example for other women *or* having an intimate, loving relationship with your man. God has no problem reconciling the two.

Maintaining a high-quality private life while you are in the public eye will not happen automatically. In fact, we have all heard too many stories of couples who "split" because one of them couldn't handle the success or

> *Being a leading lady is also the ability to move into the things God has for you without leaving behind the one who loves you.*

visibility of the other. I believe your man can be your most enthusiastic cheerleader and your most solid rock when you move into the fullness of all God has for you. When God has knit the two of you together in the intimacy of marriage, I believe His plan for you includes a crucial role for your husband. God's not leaving him out, so don't you! In order to make sure you know how to include him, I am going to devote the remainder of this chapter to helping you help him join you in the spotlight.

You're On

1. I have shared many thoughts about what a leading lady is and how she is able to keep her private life vibrant in the midst of public success. As you think specifically about your own life, what is your definition of yourself as a leading lady?

_____

_____

_____

_____

_____

_____

_____

_____

_____

_____

2. How can your man add to your ability to be a leading lady? What role or roles can he play as he takes part in your success?

_____

_____

_____

_____

_____

_____

_____

_____

_____

_____

_____

_____

_____

_____

_____

_____

_____

_____

> *The last thing we want to see is a lady who has career or ministry success, while the one thing that matters most to her goes down the tube.*

3. As I promised, I am going to devote the remainder of this chapter to helping you know how to include your man in your success. But, before I share them with you, make a list of the areas in your life that should include your man. Put an "X" next to the things that need more of your attention. Can you think of ways to include him more often? Write them down here.

_____

_____

_____

_____

_____

_____

_____

_____

_____

_____

_____

_____

_____

A man who loves you will not be satisfied to be a stagehand or a spectator at all of your shows; he will want to contribute, and he will want to stand in the spotlight with you.

Learn Your Lines

*There is no fear in love; but perfect love casts out fear,
because fear involves torment. But he who fears
has not been made perfect in love.*
1 John 4:18

*Be diligent to know the state of your flocks,
And attend to your herds;*
Proverbs 27:23

Rejoice with those who rejoice, and weep with those who weep.
Romans 12:15

Act 2: Be Careful What You Let Him See

Men are visual beings. Don't ever let it appear that, in the midst of your public success, time with him is only back-stage preparation until you're on center stage again. A man who loves you will not be satisfied to be a stagehand or a spectator at all of your shows; he will want to contribute, and he will want to stand in the spotlight with you. (If he's the shy type, call him up on stage or at least ask him to stand. That will work wonders!) Even if he is not on stage with you, he will beam when you do—not when you say, "Take out the trash before I get home."

Once you have strutted your stuff, don't always arrive home and ask for "some space." Come home and give him your undivided attention. Share your life with him—even if he doesn't respond (remember that he really wants to be

85

included). If you are depleted when you are with your man, the life will leak out of your relationship. If you always seem to need to re-charge when the two of you are together, he will soon run out of juice! Don't reserve your best performances for the boardroom or the courtroom or the operating room; save some of your best for him.

Don't leave your man in the dressing room because that is only the place where preparation takes place. Now, there is a certain level of intimacy that takes place when a man is behind-the-scenes in your life, but that intimacy is only sustained when he can come out from behind the curtain with you. He thinks, *Oh yeah, all these people are applauding her now, but they didn't see her wink at me while she was having her make-up done!* Do let him see you at your worst, but don't ever fail to let him see you at your best. Since many of you are not stage actresses or public speakers, how do these principles apply in real life?

> *Maintaining a high-quality private life while you are in the public eye will not happen automatically.*

◆ Don't allow him to see you always in your curlers, but never with a 'do.

◆ Don't allow him to watch you study, with your head buried in a book, but never ask him to attend your brilliant lecture.

◆ Don't ask him to take your car for an oil change, and then not let him ride in it.

◆ Don't ask him to sacrifice for your dreams, and then not share in them when they come true.

- Don't allow him to watch you practicing the flute and listen to your wrong notes, and then fail to have him seated front and center when you debut with the symphony.

- Don't ask him to buy you a new dress and then never wear it "just for him."

- Don't ask him to advise you, and then fail to celebrate with him when his advice results in a blessing for you.

- Don't ask him to listen to you practice your presentation, and then not tell him how it went.

You're On

1. Are you allowing your man to share your spotlight? If not, how can you begin to do that?

_____

_____

_____

_____

_____

_____

_____

_____

2. Think about the ways your man incorporates you into the various areas of his life. How does he do that? Are there areas where you would like to be more involved?

_____

_____

_____

_____

_____

_____

_____

_____

Do let him see you at your worst, but don't ever fail to let him see you at your best.

3. Now take a moment to ask your man how he would like to join you more often on center stage. What does he say?

_____

_____

_____

_____

_____

_____

_____

_____

4. What is your greatest struggle when it comes to allowing your man to step on stage with you? Are you too tired to share your life with him? Are you too busy? Do you think he wouldn't understand? How can you overcome these obstacles?

_____

_____

_____

_____

_____

_____

_____

_____

_____

_____

_____

_____

_____

_____

There is a certain level of intimacy that takes place when a man is behind-the-scenes in your life, but that intimacy is only sustained when he can come out from behind the curtain with you.

Learn Your Lines

The blessing of the Lord makes one rich,
and He adds no sorrow with it.
Proverbs 10:22

Good understanding gains favor;
but the way of the unfaithful is hard.
Proverbs 13:15

. . . through love serve one another.
Galatians 5:13

COMING SOON

*P*erhaps you walked your road to destiny alone for many years. Now, there is a man in your life. How can you share the spotlight with him? What can you look forward to as he lends his unique strengths and gifts to the role you are called to play? How can your "performance" on life's center stage be enhanced by his presence?

ACTION!

*B*ased on what you have learned in this chapter, what are three concise, measurable, attainable goals you will set for yourself as you move closer towards including your man in all that God has for you? Be sure to include a schedule and target date for reaching each goal and a reward for accomplishing it.

1. Goal: _____

Schedule and target completion date: _____

Reward: _____

_____

2. Goal: _____

Schedule and target completion date: _____

Reward: _____

_____

3. Goal: _____

Schedule and target completion date: _____

Reward: _____

_____

Notes

Notes

6

The Lady Rewards What She Wants Him to Repeat

Introducing

Emmett finally took out the trash without being asked. Gina criticized him for not doing it sooner. "You remembered," she claimed, "because the entire kitchen smelled like rotten eggs."

Emmett stopped at the dry cleaner's on his way home from work and picked up not only his shirts, but Gina's clothes as well. She didn't thank him; she only complained that they were not able to remove the stain from her silk blouse.

Emmett didn't usually shop for himself, but he took a risk one day and bought himself a new shirt. It wasn't the style he normally wore, but he liked the updated look. He put it on in preparation to attend a company dinner with Gina, but all she did was say, "You look like a fool. Go change that shirt."

Emmett took Gina's car for an oil change on Saturday morning. In an effort to surprise her, he also had it washed and detailed. "All I really needed today was a full tank of gas," she told him, "But did you get *that*? No-o-o-o-o!"

Do you know what I think? I think Emmett is about to quit doing things for Gina! You may find this hard to believe, but your man really does want to please you. Remember, men and women are like apples and oranges, so he may not know how what to do or how to do it when it comes to really pleasing you. Especially if your relationship is fairly young, he's probably on a steep learning curve. I need to tell you that the key to his success in pleasing you is not in his becoming more creative or even more sensitive; the key is in your response to his honest attempts to serve you, to surprise you, or to see you smile.

The Main Event

Act 1: If He Thinks He Can, He Will

> *If you will make a decision to reward what you want him to repeat, you'll soon see him repeat what you like.*

If you are going to be a leading lady who enjoys a transformed relationship with the man in your life, one of the smartest things you can do is understand that the behavior you reward will become the behavior he repeats. If you show him you are pleased with his actions, you'll soon see him acting in ways that please you.

You may love to share the details of your day, how God used you, what He did that day, what your thoughts were, and how you feel about it all (and your ideal is to have your man respond in the same fashion). I am going to help you understand love languages in a later chapter, but for now, let me warn you that for every three paragraphs you share with your man, expect only three words in return. While you want to love by establishing a verbal and emotional connection, he wants to love and be loved through action. But instead of criticizing what you didn't get, applaud him for what you did get and you'll be much more likely to get more of it.

How far does it get us when we complain, criticize, and get frustrated? Even if your complaints and criticisms are legitimate, have you ever moved your man to lasting, effective action with them? The next time you're ready to criticize him for his three-word response after you've poured out your insides, flip the script. After telling him every detail of your day, it's typical for you to ask him how his day was, only to have him respond with, "Oh, it was fine." But instead of taking the negative approach ("You're always giving me a superficial answer. You never share with me what's really going on") take the affirmative approach ("I really appreciate it when you share with me what's going on with you"). You may not see it in his face, but something will usually click on the inside for a man. Your acceptance of him, your appraisal of his performance, and your pleasure are more important to him than anyone else's.

Let's continue with our example of communication. By asserting or reinforcing your belief that your man is a good communicator, he can become exactly that. Men are drawn towards places where they believe they can succeed. If communicating with you is an area in which your man thinks he will fail, then communicating with you is not an area he'll

> *The next time you're ready to criticize him for his three-word response after you've poured out your insides, flip the script.*

venture towards. To change this, instead of setting him up for failure by saying what he didn't do, set him up for success by telling him how well he did. A good rule of thumb is to aim for three commendations for every criticism; keep applauding him in every way you can think of. His improvement may be gradual (he may only say five words the next time, instead of three) but the more you encourage him towards success in communication, the more he'll gravitate towards it. When a man believes he can do something competently, he will do it more often.

You're On

1. In the past, how have you criticized or complained about your man's effort to please you? How has he responded?

_____

_____

_____

_____

_____

_____

_____

_____

_____

Men are drawn towards places where they believe they can succeed.

2. What are some of the behaviors you'd like your man to exhibit more often?

_____

_____

_____

_____

_____

_____

_____

_____

_____

A good rule of thumb is to aim for three commendations for every criticism; keep applauding him in every way you can think of.

_____

_____

_____

_____

_____

_____

3. How can you immediately begin to break the pattern of critical responses and begin to reward the behavior you want him to repeat? (Hint: the next section of this chapter focuses on practical ways to reward him.)

Your verbal affirmations, as well as those knowing smiles and pats on the back, will make him feel like the man of the year.

Learn Your Lines

Then the messenger who had gone to call Micaiah spoke to him saying, "Now listen, the words of the prophets with one accord encourage the king. Please, let your words be like one of them, and speak encouragement."

1 Kings 22:13

Therefore let us pursue the things which make for peace and the things by which one may edify another.

Romans 14:19

Do all things without complaining and disputing . . .

Philippians 2:14

Act 2: How to Reward Him

One of the best ways to reward your man is to shower him with praise. Point out his strengths in every way you can think of. Your verbal affirmations, as well as those knowing smiles and pats on the back, will make him feel like the man of the year. Find ways to say something positive and encouraging to him as often as you possibly can. Compliment his choice of clothes, remark on how nice his aftershave is, notice that he cleaned out his car for you, be impressed with his knowledge of baseball statistics, commend him for taking you to such a nice restaurant, thank him for fixing the faucet, or tell him what a great dad he is. Tell him why you love him and what he means to you; tell him

Brag on him to others— especially when you know he's listening!

103

again and again and again. In your speech, include lots of "I love it when you . . ." Your success in rewarding behavior you want him to repeat will increase exponentially if you pour on the praise in front of other people. It is one thing to compliment your man while the two of you are brushing your teeth; it is something else altogether to do it while you are eating dinner with two other couples. Brag on him to others—especially when you know he's listening!

Because actions often speak louder than words for men, I want to suggest several things you might do, in addition to the positive things you might say. When dealing with your man, try to remember that accomplishment and perform- ance are supremely important in the male's world. There is something inside of him that places enormous value on win- ning, doing things right and "making it happen." For that reason, he will try extra hard to seal the deal, to win the race, to land the job, to get the promotion, to be the best. There will be times when his efforts will pay off and he will indeed conquer what- ever mountain he chose to scale. But there will also be times when, because there is only one first-place, he will not emerge victorious. In those moments, it is so important that you, as the woman in his life, be able to affirm his attempt and celebrate the fact that he tried so hard. (Trying always counts for something, you know.) Whether you prepare his favorite dinner or serve champagne at bed- time, do something to let him know that you honor his efforts and that, in your eyes, he's always number one.

> *When dealing with your man, try to remember that accomplishment and performance are supremely important in the male's world.*

Similarly, your man may have a job or another endeavor that involves long-term goals or long-range plans. If so, find a way to celebrate each milestone along the way. A project like overseeing construction on a hospital or writing a book can take a very long time, and if a person cannot celebrate as he goes, he may get discouraged and lose some of his motivation. His bosses may not ever commend him when he reaches short-range goals, but you can. Be aware of every phase he completes and applaud him every step of the way.

You're On

1. What are some areas where you know your man needs praise? How can you shower your man with verbal praise the next time you see him?

_____

_____

_____

_____

_____

_____

_____

_____

_____

_____

2. How can you use your actions rather than your words to affirm and encourage your man? List some things you can do for him.

_____

_____

_____

_____

_____

_____

_____

_____

_____

_____

_____

_____

_____

_____

_____

_____

_____

3. Celebrate a milestone and applaud an effort the next time it is appropriate. How do you think this will affect your relationship with your man? Do you think this will affect his view of himself? His view of you?

_____

_____

_____

_____

_____

_____

_____

_____

_____

_____

_____

_____

_____

_____

_____

_____

Whether you prepare his favorite dinner or serve champagne at bedtime, do something to let him know that you honor his efforts and that, in your eyes, he's always number one.

Learn Your Lines

Pleasant words are like a honeycomb,
sweetness to the soul and health to the bones.
Proverbs 16:24

So I perceived that nothing is better than that a man
should rejoice in his own works, for that is his heritage.
Ecclesiastes 3:22a

Therefore I urge you to reaffirm your love to him.
2 Corinthians 2:8

COMING SOON

$\mathcal{C}$an you imagine what would happen if you began to reward the behavior you want your man to repeat? Let me be clear: we are not talking about manipulation, so don't go down that road as you look ahead. We are talking about genuine affirmation, edification, and encouragement. Think about the difference these behaviors will make when you receive them. What kind of difference do you think they will make in your man? Think about how much your intimacy and enjoyment of life will improve as he gains confidence in his ability to please you (which is what he really longs to do!)

ACTION!

Based on what you have learned in this chapter, what are three concise, measurable, attainable goals you will set for yourself as you learn to reward the behavior you want him to repeat and pour out the praise on your man? Be sure to include a schedule and target date for reaching each goal and a reward for accomplishing it.

1. Goal: _____

Schedule and target completion date: _____

Reward: _____

_____

2. Goal: _____

Schedule and target completion date: _____

Reward: _____

_____

3. Goal: _____

Schedule and target completion date: _____

Reward: _____

_____

Notes

Notes

7

The Lady Knows How to Talk to Her Man, Part 1

Introducing

et's say a married couple plans to go out to dinner on Friday night. They don't know which restaurant they will go to, but when Friday night rolls around, the husband says, "I'm want to take you somewhere you'll really like."

She says to him, "How about Chinese?"

He says, "No, we always have Chinese because that's my favorite. Tonight, we're having Italian."

She protests and suggests a nice Chinese restaurant. He persists with his idea to eat Italian.

They ate Italian, but neither one went home satisfied. Why? Because on Wednesday night, she commented, "I sure would like some good Italian food," and he made a mental note. But by the time Friday rolled around, she really had a taste for Chinese. He *thought* her suggestion to eat Chinese was an effort to please him because she never made it clear that her hunger for Italian food on Wednesday had been replaced by a genuine desire for Chinese on Friday. She *thought* he was the one who wanted Italian, when in reality he had shifted his own taste buds away from Chinese in order to make her happy. In the end, they didn't communicate clearly, and she didn't ask his opinion on the matter.

The Main Event

Act 1: Using Words Effectively

Because you, leading lady, are most likely a verbal communicator, I would like to first address communication in terms of the way you and your man speak to each other. I encourage you to learn to communicate more and more by your actions, since your man gravitates towards that. But speech will always be an essential part of communication, so I also want you to learn to use your words effectively. Any intimate relationship involves a longing—on the part of both the lady and the gentleman—to be understood. There are times when one person has the "gift of gab" and will use many words to truly communicate very little, but expect that the sheer volume of words uttered has resulted in understanding. There are also situations in which one person will verbalize very little, but assume nevertheless that he or she is somehow being understood. Both strategies produce ambiguity, perhaps in an attempt to avoid disagreement. In the end, where clarity is missing, confusion reigns.

Where clarity is missing, confusion reigns.

Earlier in this workbook, we dealt with some of the differences between men and women. No matter how head-over-heels in love you are, you and your man are still two distinct individuals with two different perspectives, two different approaches to conflict resolution, and two different styles of communication. That's why clarity is so important; it really is necessary that you say what you mean and mean what you say. When clarity exists, even two distinct individuals can work together to make a good decision or resolve a situation. As you move towards greater clarity in your communication in your intimate relationship, you might consider the ten recommendations below. Every one of them will not apply to every situation in which you find yourself, but they do include several of the important points of clarity you will want to be aware of and address in your verbal interaction with the man you love.

◆ Make sure the *issues* are clear.

◆ Make sure your *intentions* are clear.

◆ Make sure your *preferences* are clear.

◆ Make sure the *risks* are clear.

◆ Make sure the *consequences* are clear.

◆ Make sure your *expectations* are clear.

◆ Make sure the *points of agreement and disagreement* are clear.

◆ Make sure the *plan* is clear.

◆ Make sure the *purpose* is clear. (In other words, know why you are discussing what you are discussing).

◆ Make sure the *questions* are clear. (Sometimes the right answer only comes when you ask the right questions).

The care you must give to your words and the accountability that clarity breeds will not only enhance your communication but also strengthen your bond with each other.

Now, I understand that clarity can sometimes feel self-ish or feel like overkill. You may feel less than generous if you are constantly telling your man what you want, or feel that you are stating the obvious when you comment on a situation. Deal with the discomfort; it's far better than the disappointment and disagreement that can result from assumptions or uncertainties.

Clarity is not the only important ingredient in communicating with your man. Other components include kindness, proper timing, putting an issue in context, and speaking the truth in love. Nevertheless, clarity is a critical element that will cause you to think about what you say and then make you accountable. The care you must give to your words and the accountability that clarity generates will not only enhance your communication, but strengthen your bond with each other.

> *No matter how head-over-heels in love you are, you and your man are still two distinct individuals with two different perspectives, two different approaches to conflict resolution, and two different styles of communication. That's why clarity is so important.*

You're On

1. Can you remember situations where lack of clarity caused frustration, confusion, or conflict in your relationship with your man? Why do you think the two of you were reluctant to express yourselves clearly during those times?

_____

_____

_____

_____

_____

_____

_____

_____

_____

_____

_____

_____

_____

There are times when it's best to tell him what the point is, stay focused on it, and use as few words as possible!

2. What can you do to begin to incorporate more clarity into your communication with your man?

_____

_____

_____

_____

_____

_____

_____

_____

_____

_____

_____

_____

_____

_____

_____

_____

_____

When you want to use colorful language and figures of speech and speak in long, eloquent sentences—or paragraphs—find a woman to talk to.

3. How do you think clarity will enhance your relationship?

_____
_____
_____
_____
_____
_____
_____
_____
_____
_____
_____
_____
_____
_____
_____
_____
_____
_____
_____

A man wants you to make your point clearly and succinctly, without getting sidetracked by too many details.

Learn Your Lines

Plans are established by counsel; by wise counsel wage war.
Proverbs 20:18

But let your "Yes" be "Yes," and your "No," "No."
Matthew 5:37a

Act 2: Get to the Point

Have you ever watched a group of men play basketball? It is an amazing phenomenon from a woman's point of view. They never introduce themselves (or if they do, it's last name only; they refer to each other as "Man" or "Bro"), and they understand a whole language of grunts that is unintelligible to women! They pass, dribble, and shoot, with 99% of their focus on the ball. The 1% of their attention that is given to the other players is done so only because they need someone to pass the ball to! When they finish the game, they clap and cheer and give each other high-fives; then they talk about what a great time they had together and make plans to do it again next Sunday afternoon.

To a man, that's communication. Everybody knew the point; they were all there to get the ball through the hoop more times than the other team could. And best of all, everybody stayed focused on the point of the game. To be honest with you, the basketball game is a good illustration of the way a man likes to communicate. There are times when it's best to tell him what the point is, stay focused on it, and use as few words as possible! When you want to use colorful language and figures of speech and speak in long, eloquent sentences—or paragraphs—find a woman to talk to. When you want to engage in the art of conversation for conversation's sake, find a female. When you want have a cup of tea and "chat," you'll do best to seek out someone of your own gender.

I am writing partly in jest, but the truth of the matter is that a man wants you to make your point clearly and succinctly, without getting sidetracked by too many details. You see, a man gets nervous when he does not know where you are going with your train of words. Communicating with him works best when you state your point first and then add the peripheral information later. When you begin to speak to him, start by letting him know exactly what your conversation is really about. Otherwise, your man will be trying to figure out the point, based on your details, and he can get very confused. He is thinking, *So does she want a blue dress because Yvette had a blue dress or does she want to make those little appetizers for the next party we throw?* When in fact, the only reason you mentioned Yvette's blue dress and the delicious appetizers was to eventually tell him that Yvette, who brought those appetizers, hit your car as she was leaving the party and now your fender is in the backseat.

The more effective way to communicate with him is to say, "The car got hit today and the fender is in the backseat." Deal with that situation, and mention the appetizers later. By the time you've finished, you yourself may not even care about Yvette's dress!

> *A man gets nervous when he does not know where you are going with your train of words.*

Even when your conversation focuses on an issue that is less dramatic than the fender, start with the main point, present it with clarity and trickle down to the details. He will be better able to stay with you, and even though he may not respond the way you'd like, he is more likely to pay attention to everything you say. When you start with the core issue, he knows the real substance of the discussion, and you can be sure he's tracking it with you.

You're On

1. Have you talked to your man about details before you got to the point of a conversation? How did those conversations usually end? List a few instances that come to mind.

2. What do you think you can do to help you make your point first and deal with details later? Don't you think that using self-discipline to hold back details until you've stated your point will tremendously improve communication with the man in your life?

_____

_____

_____

_____

_____

_____

_____

_____

_____

_____

_____

_____

_____

_____

_____

_____

3. Try to remember times when you and your man had excellent communication. Write down what you can remember about those times. Now, try to remember if there were any common denominators during each of those times? Write them down.

_____

_____

_____

_____

_____

_____

_____

_____

_____

_____

_____

_____

_____

_____

_____

_____

_____

Learn Your Lines

He who has knowledge spares his words,
and a man of understanding is of a calm spirit.
Proverbs 17:27

The tongue of the wise uses knowledge rightly,
but the mouth of fools pours forth foolishness.
Proverbs 15:2

Listen to counsel and receive instruction,
that you may be wise in your latter days.
Proverbs 19:20

COMING SOON

*A*s you look forward to being able to better communicate with the one you love, what hopes do you have for your relationship? What mutual understandings do you hope the two of you can reach? How can you more clearly articulate your dreams and aspirations for the future? How can you apply the lessons you've learned about clarity to make your point to your man before delving into details?

_____

_____

_____

_____

_____

_____

_____

_____

_____

_____

_____

_____

ACTION!

Based on what you have learned in this chapter, what are three concise, measurable, attainable goals you will set for yourself as you work to improve your communication skills, so that you can be clear and focus on your point, rather than on details? Be sure to include a schedule and target date for reaching each goal and a reward for accomplishing it.

1. Goal: _____

Schedule and target completion date: _____

Reward: _____

_____

2. Goal: _____

Schedule and target completion date: _____

Reward: _____

_____

3. Goal: _____

Schedule and target completion date: _____

Reward: _____

_____

Notes

8

The Lady Knows How to Talk to Her Man, Part 2

Introducing

Now that you are learning about the importance of making your point clearly when you communicate with your man, in this chapter I want us to further explore your style of communication. Along with the many adjustments a woman needs to make when she is involved in an intimate relationship with a man, she may need to alter some of the ways she expresses herself. Especially if the leading lady is accustomed to speaking often and with authority in professional settings, she may have to be silent at times, so that her beloved feels free to express himself. In other words, don't make it possible for the man you love to truthfully tell his buddies, "That woman talks so much I can't get a word in edgewise!"

On the other hand, you may be a leading lady who spends much of her time listening, or is naturally quiet and reserved.

In that case, you will need to adjust by learning to speak up and make your thoughts and feelings known.

While you are at it, may I suggest one more adjustment that may prove a bit challenging (but well worth it) to those leading ladies who relish their independence and enjoy being able to think for themselves? I strongly recommend that you incorporate this question into your communication, and ask it often: "What do you think?" I can hear you now. You may be saying to yourself, "But I already know what I should do," or "Asking his opinion will only slow me down!" Do it anyway; you are not trying to win a race with your communication style and skill. You are trying to increase intimacy with the one you love.

The Main Event

Act 1: The Speakers and the Hearers

We can analyze communication styles in many ways, from many different angles, but at the most fundamental level, people are usually either speakers or hearers. Some like to talk; some prefer to listen. You wonder why some even have a set of ears, and you wonder if others open their mouths for any purpose besides eating and teeth brushing. Many times, an intimate relationship will be composed of one talker and one listener, so it becomes crucial that both learn to adapt to the style of the other in order for their communication to be effective.

If you, leading lady, are a listener, you've probably learned a lot. Listeners are prone to hearing the words spoken and pondering what they've heard. They also tend to remember things people have said. Somewhere in your past, you may have heard maxims such as "Silence is golden" or "You have two ears and one mouth, so listen twice as much as you talk."

In a relationship, I'm not sure that listening twice as much as you talk is good advice to follow. You see, as one who listens, you may fail to share yourself with your man by saying what you need to say—and that means he doesn't *really* know you. He may not know what you really like, what you don't like, or how you process events and emotions. Your words give powerful insight into who you are, and your deep mutual knowledge of one another makes intimacy possible.

We can analyze communication styles in many ways, from many different angles, but at the most fundamental level, people are usually either speakers or hearers.

If you have spent most of your relationship being quiet and not sharing much, here is a brief list of things to make sure you tell your man. It represents a variety of topics from the silly to the serious, but I hope that you will find these ideas to be not only useful in and of themselves, but also good thought-starters for more insights you might want to share about yourself.

- your favorite perfume
- your favorite restaurant
- your best childhood memory
- your most beloved Christmas tradition
- the name of a childhood pet
- your favorite love song
- your thoughts as you began to fall in love with him

- your hopes, dreams, and aspirations

- your favorite book

- the thing you most respect about him

- the quality you would most like to be remembered for

- a hobby you'd like to try or a skill you'd like to develop

> *Your words give powerful insight into who you are, and your deep mutual knowledge of one another makes intimacy possible.*

On the other hand, if you talk a lot, then a truly intimate relationship will require that you close your mouth sometimes and use your ears. Even if you are a talker, you may also be the best listener in his life. Use your words to ask questions, and then pay attention to your man's answers. That's the way to understand him—and he really longs to be understood. I want to encourage you to begin listening with both your ears and your heart; hear not only what he says, but what he feels. You may have heard the principles of active listening before, as they are fairly common, but I'll summarize them for you here.

- Encourage him by looking him in the eye, nodding your head and occasionally saying, "yes" and "I'm listening" (and meaning it).

- Ask questions so that you can be sure you clearly understand him.

◆ Use phrases like "What I hear you saying is . . ." and "So what you're saying is . . ." Then repeat what you believe you heard so that you are hearing his words and getting the message behind them correctly. Give him a chance to clarify if you do not understand.

◆ Continue to nod, smile when appropriate, and say "yes," "I hear you" and send other verbal and non-verbal signs that you are hearing him and paying attention.

You're On

1. Are you a speaker or a hearer? Is the man in your life a speaker or hearer? How does this work out for both of you? Do you need to do more of one and less of another? Explain.

_____

_____

_____

_____

_____

_____

Ask questions, and then pay attention to your man's answers. That's the way to understand him—and he really longs to be understood.

_____

_____

2. Describe a specific time when it was better to be more of a speaker in a relationship. And then describe a specific time when it was better to be more of a hearer.

Being able to articulate his point of view is an important element of communication for a man.

3. The principles of active listening are good for everyone, speakers and hearers alike (some hearers are just quiet; they aren't necessarily excellent listeners!). What did you learn as you read them and how can you incorporate it into your style of communication so that you are balancing speaking with active listening?

_____

_____

_____

_____

_____

_____

_____

_____

_____

_____

_____

_____

_____

When you are interested enough to request your man's viewpoint on an issue, he feels valued and affirmed.

Learn Your Lines

*Let the words of my mouth and the meditation
of my heart be acceptable in Your sight, O Lord,
my strength and my Redeemer.*
Psalm 19:14

*The words of a man's mouth are deep waters;
the wellspring of wisdom is a flowing brook.*
Proverbs 18:4

*The heart of the prudent acquires knowledge,
and the ear of the wise seeks knowledge.*
Proverbs 18:15

*Apply your heart to instruction,
and your ears to words of knowledge.*
Proverbs 23:12

Act 2: A Very Important Question

Chances are, your man has his own opinions—maybe
lots of opinions, and maybe more than you care to think
about. But let me tell you something about men: they really,
really want to be able to express those opinions. Being able
to articulate his point of view is an important element of
communication for him, and even if you are a speaker—
especially if you are a speaker, learning to ask his opinion
and to hear it is one of the best moves you can make. It isn't

necessary to a man for others to agree with him; he simply wants to tell others what he thinks and have his opinion respected and not ridiculed. Now, I am not simply encouraging you to ask his opinion on the national news or the famine in Africa or the economic woes in South America. I am talking about consulting him with the everyday matters of your life together. Ask him things like:

◆ "What do you think we should have for dinner — chicken or fish?"

◆ "How do you think I could best invest this extra money I've earned?"

◆ "What color flowers do you think I should plant on the patio?"

◆ "How do you think we should spend the long weekend coming up?"

◆ "What do you think we should get Junior for his birthday?"

◆ "What time do you think we should leave for the concert?"

◆ "Which dress do you think is more appropriate for your office party — the green one or the red one?"

> *Your man will not always tell you what you want to hear, but when that happens, take the time to evaluate what he's said.*

When you are interested enough to request his viewpoint on an issue, he feels valued and affirmed. What he says in response to you is far less important than the fact that you cared enough to ask.

Your man will not always tell you what you want to hear, but when that happens, take the time to evaluate what he's said. There is a possibility that his opinion will make you aware of an additional option or a potential pitfall you had not considered. At other times, you will blatantly disagree with him, and you will have to decide how to handle that. I can only encourage you to choose your battles wisely. When you ask for his opinion, you are trying to build him up, not tear him down. One wise response is, "Thanks. I'll think about that." Then, you can go back later and say, "I decided to do this instead." A whole, healthy man will not feel rejected; he'll be glad you sought his advice and deemed it worthy of consideration.

You're On

1. When was the last time you looked at your man and said, "What do you think . . .?" How did he respond?

_____

_____

_____

_____

_____

_____

_____

_____

_____

2. What do you need to do in order to remember to ask his opinion more often? How can you benefit from his perspective?

_____

_____

_____

_____

_____

_____

_____

_____

_____

_____

_____

_____

_____

_____

_____

_____

_____

3. How will you handle situations when his opinion is not what you wanted to hear?

Learn Your Lines

A wise man will hear and increase in learning,
and a man of understanding will attain wise counsel.
Proverbs 1:5

Apply your heart to instruction,
and your ears to words of knowledge.
Proverbs 23:12

COMING SOON

 really believe you want the best communication you can possibly have with your man. How can the principles you've read about in this chapter improve the way you relate to each other as you learn to strike the right balance between speaking and hearing, and as you allow your man opportunities to express his opinion? What positive changes do you believe can take place as you apply these lessons?

_____

_____

_____

_____

_____

_____

_____

_____

_____

_____

_____

_____

_____

ACTION!

*B*ased on what you have learned in this chapter, what are three concise, measurable, attainable goals you will set for yourself when it comes to the choice of speaking or listening? Be sure to include a schedule and target date for reaching each goal and a reward for accomplishing it.

1. Goal: _____

Schedule and target completion date: _____

Reward: _____

_____

2. Goal: _____

Schedule and target completion date: _____

Reward: _____

_____

3. Goal: _____

Schedule and target completion date: _____

Reward: _____

_____

Notes

9

The Lady Accepts and Allows

Introducing

Roberta and George have been married for years and, over time, they have both mellowed. In the early days of the relationship, George was not sure how long he would last—not because he didn't love Roberta, but because every Sunday afternoon, all she could talk about was Reverend Jackson.

"George," she would say, "We need to find out where Reverend Jackson gets his ties. Don't you think he has such pretty ties? We need to get you some ties like Reverend Jackson's."

If it wasn't his ties, it was his hair or his beard. "George, why don't you go down to that barber shop where Reverend Jackson goes? That barber could probably cut your hair just like the Reverend's."

If it wasn't something to do with his appearance, it was his personality. "George, you know that Reverend Jackson is so funny! He tells such funny stories when he visits our Sunday school class. Oh, he just makes me nearly split my skirt laughing! Don't you know any funny stories, George?"

If it wasn't a personality flaw, it was spiritual. "George, I just love how Reverend Jackson knows the Word. I mean, that man can speak the language of Zion! That King James scripture just rolls off his lips like honey. And it makes me want to be a better person. Yes, it does. George, you ought to read your Bible more and memorize some stuff. You have a good voice, and you just need to start quoting some scripture."

See what I mean? George thought about praying that Reverend Jackson would find another place to pastor, but he couldn't bear the thought of Roberta's moaning and groaning once Reverend Perfect was gone. So he learned to grunt periodically while Roberta raved—and he learned to go fishing on Sundays.

Eventually, Reverend Jackson fell from grace, and once Roberta recovered from the disappointment, she realized that stable, steady, not funny, ugly-tie George was a pretty good guy after all. Over time, she quit nagging him because it wasn't doing any good. But over time, George changed. He didn't turn into Reverend Jackson, but he did become a man she couldn't help falling in love with day after day after day.

The Main Event

Act 1: Accepting Your Man

Everybody wants to be accepted. In fact, one of the most subtle and insidious forms of rejecting someone is to constantly demand that they change. Sometimes, the demands are unspoken or presented as a compliment (we'll get to that later in this chapter), but they can be felt. Any time you wish your man would change in any way, you are failing to truly accept him—and that will prevent true intimacy and undermine many of the positive aspects of your relationship.

If you are not currently in an intimate relationship, one of the most important pieces of advice I can give you is to be brutally realistic as you consider becoming involved with a man. By "brutally realistic," I mean that you need to make an honest appraisal of who he is, not a romantic prediction of who you *think* he can be. In order to have a relationship that is based in reality, you must accept him for who he is right this minute. Don't make the mistake of falling in love with potential. Never stop thinking the best of people; never stop believing in them, but when it comes to spending your life with a man in an intimate relationship, be sure you're happy with who you've got, not with what you hope he'll become.

If you are married and find yourself wishing your husband would change—and you are trying to make him—stop. Change is always an option, and progress is always possible, but most men will resist fiercely as long as they feel they are being forced. Relax, and let him be who he is. After all, he was good enough for you to marry, wasn't he?

Married or not, one key to accepting the man in your life is to refuse to compare him to anyone else. All of the praise and positive reinforcement you can give will be seriously diluted if you mix it with comparison. Unless a woman is angry or trying to stir up trouble, she often uses a comparison as a compliment. Most men, on the other hand, don't see comparison as flattering or honoring in the least. You see, a

> *Any time you wish your man would change in any way, you are failing to truly accept him—and that will prevent true intimacy and undermine many of the positive aspects of your relationship.*

man so values his individuality that he is in no way compli-mented when you say, "You know, you remind me so much of So-and-So!" or "You are just like my pastor / father / work associate / old boyfriend!" or "Oh, you cook those steaks on the grill the same way Alvin does!" Instead, he may hear a veiled demand that he be more like So-and So or a hint that he is not really acceptable to you. He may feel that you are asking him to live up to a standard he can't reach, or isn't interested in pursuing. If he does not like the man to whom you've compared him, he'll be downright offended! He wants the freedom to be himself and the assurance that you accept him completely, never try-ing to see how he measures up to anyone else.

Let me also say that the fastest way to cause tension between two men is to com-pare them. If you insist upon telling your man how much he reminds you of your pastor (even if that is the world's highest compliment in your mind), do not be sur-prised if he resists going to church with you. If you compare him to your older brother, who always protected you and made you feel so safe, then he may let you go to Thanksgiving dinner alone so that you can feel so safe with your brother. Your man treasures his uniqueness, so be sure you treasure and affirm it too.

Finally, as you are learning to accept your man, I would like to give you two pieces of advice. First, leave his stuff

> *Don't make the mistake of falling in love with potential. Never stop thinking the best of people; never stop believing in them, but when it comes to spending your life with a man in an intimate relationship, be sure you're happy with the man you've got, not with the man you hope he'll become.*

alone! And second, let him have some secrets (I am not talking about deception, lies, or "hiding." I am talking about his harmless, private thoughts that do not hinder in any way your growing intimacy or ability to share deeply.) Women don't normally warm to the idea of "butting out," but I am telling you that a man feels extremely comfortable and accepted by a woman who is not nosy or suspicious. His belongings mark his personal territory, and his secrets represent his mental or emotional space. He wants to know you trust him enough to not snoop in his drawers or pry into the recesses of his mind. He's really not too different from you in that regard, is he?

You're On

1. List some of the things about your man that you wish you could change, even though you must know you can never change him. In what ways are you silently or subtly rejecting your man by wishing he would change?

_____

_____

_____

_____

_____

_____

_____

2. How can you better accept him—not just in your words and deeds, but in your heart and mind? How can you affirm his uniqueness?

_____
_____
_____
_____
_____
_____
_____
_____
_____
_____
_____
_____
_____
_____

One key to accepting the man in your life is to refuse to compare him to anyone else. All of the praise and positive reinforcement you can give will be seriously diluted if you mix it with comparison.

3. If you tend to pry into your man's life or are nosy, how can you accept that fact that you really do need to stay out of his stuff and let him have some secrets? (Hint: this is going to require an increase in trust!) How would you feel if your man was nosy and suspicious of you?

> *Women don't normally warm to the idea of "butting out," but I am telling you that a man feels extremely comfortable and accepted by a woman who is not nosy or suspicious.*

Learn Your Lines

Blessed be the God and Father of our Lord Jesus Christ, who has blessed us with every spiritual blessing in the heavenly places in Christ, just as He chose us in Him before the foundation of the world, that we should be holy and without blame before Him in love, having predestined us to adoption as sons by Christ Jesus to Himself, according to the good pleasure of His will, to the praise of the glory of His grace, by which He made us accepted in the Beloved.

Ephesians 1:3-6

Coming to Him as a living stone, rejected indeed by men, but chosen by God and precious . . .

1 Peter 2:4

Act 2: Allowing Transformation

One of the decisions I encourage a leading lady to make is to decide that you cannot *transform* your man, you can only *inform* him. Transformation—the process of deep and lasting change—is not something one human being can do for another, and as you've already learned, wanting and trying to change him will not serve the relationship well and can, in fact, cause damage.

Nevertheless, intimate relationships are environments in which we see the need for change both in ourselves and in those we love. But I need to tell you that being in a close relationship gives you neither the responsibility nor the right to try to transform the man you love. That is God's job; not yours.

What you can do is *inform* him, as long as you do so without guile, without an ulterior motive, without attempting to manipulate. You can share your observations, your knowledge, or your experience in a way that simply communicates, "This is something that's worked for me . . ." or "Another way to approach this situation might be to . . ." or "I've known some other people who dealt with that and they overcame by . . ." At the same time, continue to affirm your man and keep conveying your acceptance of who he is right now.

Too often, a woman takes on an extra responsibility (such as getting her man to change) that eventually wears her out. She says what's on their mind and then tries to get him to agree with her point. That won't work; he has a mind of his own. Your best bet is to state your information, speak the truth in love, and let your man and God deal with the facts the way they want to.

Furthermore, I have come to believe that one of the great disservices we human beings perform for one another is to try to make life easy. Women who are mercy-motivated, wounded or desperate can be the worst! They will go to extremes, even to their own detriment, to keep a man from suffering the consequences of his choices or bearing the weight of his responsibilities. They behave this way primarily because they are afraid he will leave if they don't.

When you love someone, his comfort is really not your top priority: his development is. Real love wants to see a

> *One of the decisions I encourage a leading lady to make is to recognize that you **cannot** transform **your man**, you can only inform **him**.*

man grow, even if growth requires stretching and some pain along the way. Real love will allow a man to mature, to develop discipline, to make mistakes (because that's how he learns), and to deal with the fallout of those mistakes. Real love does not act like a fortress, shielding him from hostile fire, nor does it act like an ambulance, always rushing to his rescue with medicine to numb the pain. No, if you love him, you will allow him life's necessary sufferings; you will allow him to learn to walk when his legs are broken—because that's the way he gets stronger.

> *Your best bet is to state your information, speak the truth in love, and let your man and God deal with the facts the way they want to.*

I challenge you to be committed to your man's personal development and maturity. Stop trying to shield him from the redemptive pain or the productive challenges that present themselves. Being a champion for his growth will require that you be straight up honest, that you say what he *needs* to hear instead of what he *wants* to hear. By doing so, you allow him to be transformed according to the pace and process God has designed for him.

You're On

1. Are you guilty of trying to change your man? How can you begin to inform without attempting to transform?

_____

_____

_____

_____

_____

_____

_____

_____

_____

_____

_____

_____

_____

_____

_____

_____

_____

When you love someone, his comfort is really not your top priority: his development is.

2. Are you one who tries to make your man's life easy and struggle-free? List some of the instances when you did exactly that. How has that hindered his development or maturity?

_____

_____

_____

_____

_____

_____

_____

_____

_____

_____

_____

_____

_____

_____

_____

_____

3. How can you begin to allow the man in your life to go through what he needs to experience in order to grow?

_____

_____

_____

_____

_____

_____

_____

_____

_____

_____

_____

_____

_____

_____

_____

Being a champion for his growth will require that you be straight up honest, that you say what he needs to hear instead of what he wants to hear.

Learn Your Lines

*And not only that, but we also glory in tribulations,
knowing that tribulation produces perseverance;
and perseverance, character; and character, hope.*
Romans 5:3, 4

*But we all, with unveiled face, beholding as in a mirror the
glory of the Lord, are being transformed into the same image
from glory to glory, just as by the Spirit of the Lord.*
2 Corinthians 3:18

*My brethren, count it all joy when you fall into various trials,
knowing that the testing of your faith produces patience.*
James 1:2, 3

COMING SOON

$\mathcal{C}$an you imagine the tension that will disappear when you begin to accept your man for who he is, refuse to compare him with anyone else, and stop trying to change him? Chances are, your joy will increase and your ability to relax and have fun together will skyrocket. What do you think?

ACTION!

$\mathcal{B}$ased on what you have learned in this chapter, what are three concise, measurable, attainable goals you will set for yourself in the area of accepting your man just the way he is and sharing information or advice with him for the purpose of informing him, not transforming him? Be sure to include a schedule and target date for reaching each goal and a reward for accomplishing it.

1. Goal: _____

Schedule and target completion date: _____

Reward: _____

_____

2. Goal: _____

Schedule and target completion date: _____

Reward: _____

_____

3. Goal: _____

Schedule and target completion date: _____

Reward: _____

_____

Notes

Notes

10

The Lady Handles Conflict Well

Introducing

The good times you and your man experience do not make or break your relationship. Laughing together, as healthy and wonderful as it is, isn't likely to test your character, and in the midst of smiles and chuckles, no one is apt to get his or her feathers ruffled. No, when we think about building and maintaining strong, intimate relationships, it is the angry moments that are most dangerous. It is when tempers rage and emotions are on edge that two people who really do love each other can damage one another. Unkind words can deeply wound a person's heart. The "silent treatment" can leave the person you love confused and frustrated—especially when the silent one emerges and says something like, "Just let it go. I've dealt with it. I don't want to talk about it anymore; let's just go on."

For this reason, you need to be equipped to understand conflict and deal with it productively when it blows in like a winter storm. Conflict will come, but if you can learn and begin to incorporate the principles in this chapter, you will be well on your way towards managing it successfully, having less destruction to deal with in its wake, and being able to move forward with greater freedom and wholeness.

The Main Event

Act 1: Fight a Good Fight

When I wrote to you about the importance of asking for your man's opinions and respecting them, I let you know (as if you don't already!) that his opinions will not always match yours. Beyond differing opinions, you will also have full-blown disagreements because the fact that you love each other does not mean you will always see eye-to-eye or that you will never have reason to argue. In any intimate relationship, conflict is inevitable, but it does not have to be destructive. Therefore, you must find ways to disagree without causing damage.

Let me share with you how men view conflict and differences of opinion. When a man disagrees with someone, or someone disagrees with him, his logical brain shifts into overdrive. While you may fear an argument, he is fascinated by it. He sees it as less of a crisis and more of a challenge. It is less of a stumbling block or an obstacle to intimacy than it is an opportunity for him to state his case, justify assertions, support his reasoning and engage in a brilliant moment of oratory as he closes his argument. You see, there is something about a man's performance orientation and his compelling need to excel that just can't resist a good disagreement. If you understand this, you can take the conflict less personally and help minimize the damage. That's how you fight a *good* fight and not a bad one.

> *In any intimate relationship, conflict is inevitable, but it does not have to be destructive.*

172

Disagreements don't need to end in feelings of being devalued, mocked, or attacked. They should not become painful, and they don't need to be such bad experiences that you end up avoiding them just to keep the peace. It is okay to disagree. It is okay to maintain your own opinion and for that opinion to differ from your man's. It is *not* okay for your disagreements to cause damage to either party—physically, emotionally or mentally.

Here are some pointers to help you disagree without being destructive:

◆ Recognize in the beginning that a difference of opinion is not a personal affront to you.

◆ Do not raise your voice or allow yourself to lapse into a sarcastic tone.

◆ Don't accuse. Use "I" statements rather than "you" statements.

◆ Keep your body language open and attentive, not defensive.

◆ Do not use the words "always" and "never." They imply perfection, which human beings just don't attain. Statements including those words beg to be defended.

◆ Remember that one person does not have to "win." The object is for both of you to be heard and respected.

◆ Don't insist upon resolution of every conflict. There will be times you can agree to disagree and still live happily ever after.

It is okay to disagree; it is okay to hold your own opinion and for that opinion to differ from your man's; it is not okay for your disagreements to cause damage to either party—physically, emotionally or mentally.

> *Some issues are not worthy of your time and energy because there is little, if any, value to be gained or progress to be made by investing in them.*

Now, having tried to ensure that you know how to disagree without causing damage, I also want to make sure you know that some wars simply are not worth waging. Some issues are not worth your time and energy because there is little, if any, value to be gained or progress to be made by investing your thoughts and words and emotions in them. I have written, concerning such conflicts, that, "They provide lots of fireworks, but no heat and lasting light" (*How to Love a Black Man,* p. 99). Therefore, let them fizzle.

Listed below are several indicators that a conflict is not worth your engagement in it and that you should let it go.

◆ Let it go when it is not the result of a difference of opinion, but of fatigue or stress or some other external source not related to the issue.

◆ Let it go when its resolution will not advance an important purpose, increase your understanding of one another in order to build intimacy, or demolish an obstacle to progress that the two of you have committed to make.

◆ Let it go when one of you is feeling needy or weak — and is therefore trying to "win."

◆ Let it go when the matter over which you are arguing is trivial anyway.

◆ Let it go when one of you is "just being difficult."

◆ Let it go when the argument is being used for emotional manipulation.

◆ Let it go when it is being used to mask a larger or genuinely important matter.

Even in the best of relationships, disagreements will occur, but I believe that you can handle them in the spirit of a true leading lady who knows how to make conflict constructive instead of destructive, and who is strong enough and wise enough to let some potentially volatile situations simply fizzle out.

You're On

1. How would you characterize the conflict management skills in your relationship with your man? Do you need to learn how to disagree without causing damage?

_____

_____

_____

_____

_____

_____

_____

_____

2. In your own words, based on your knowledge of your unique and special relationship with your man, how would you define a constructive disagreement? How would you describe a destructive disagreement? Once you've answered this question, you may have more specific items to add to my list of things that will help your disagreements not cause damage.

_____

_____

_____

_____

_____

Because there are no perfect people, there is no perfect relationship.

_____

_____

_____

_____

_____

_____

_____

_____

9. Do you jump in to fight every battle that arises? How can you learn to choose wisely which arguments you will engage in and which you will allow to fizzle out?

_____

_____

_____

_____

_____

_____

_____

_____

_____

_____

_____

_____

_____

_____

_____

_____

I believe that you can handle disagreements in the spirit of a true leading lady who knows how to make conflict constructive instead of destructive, and who is strong enough and wise enough to let some potentially volatile situations simply fizzle out.

Learn Your Lines

Better to dwell in the wilderness,
than with a contentious and angry woman.
Proverbs 21:19

Make no friendship with an angry man,
and with a furious man do not go, lest you learn his ways
and set a snare for your soul.
Proverbs 22:24-25

"Be angry and do not sin": do not let the sun go down
on your wrath, nor give place to the devil.
Ephesians 4:26, 27

Act 2: Forgive and Finish It

Have you ever met a perfect person—not someone who thinks he or she is perfect, but someone who really is? I didn't think so. Because there are no perfect people, there is no perfect relationship, and no matter how proficient you become in your conflict management skills and how many battles you allow to fizzle out, you and the man you love will inevitably say something hurtful or do something that causes pain. So it's important that you know how to apologize, how to forgive, and how to finish a situation for good.

Apologies are not easy for most people. In fact, some people nearly choke when they even think about saying, "I'm sorry." We say those words, most of the time because we feel we must—or should. An apology requires a big breath of humility; it hurts our egos; and it is tantamount to admitting fault.

The key to apologizing well to a man is to make your apology action-oriented and not focused on emotions. Admit your guilt in specific terms, and then let him know how you plan to keep from repeating your transgression. For instance, "I am so sorry I taped over the Super Bowl. Next time I get ready to record a show, I'll get a new tape."

At the same time, receiving an apology can be just as difficult as saying, "I'm sorry." When you've been genuinely hurt—and your man is admitting that he hurt you, because he is apologizing—you may want to bleed or whimper or lick your wounds for a while. In addition, you might not want to let him off the hook with nothing more than the mere utterance of two words.

The truth is that a man is quite challenged by the need to apologize—not necessarily because he thinks he's right, but because he is afraid you may think less of him if he admits to a fault. And remember, he can't stand the thought of not pleasing you.

Just as an action-oriented apology is most effective when dealing with a man, accepting his apology with a commitment to action is equally important. To him, your willingness to make progress in the area of offense brings substance to your emotions. For instance, once he has offered you a genuine apology, respond by saying something like, "I accept your apology. What do you think we can do to keep this from happening again?"

> *The key to apologizing well to a man is to make your apology action-oriented and not focused on emotions.*

Now, even more critical than learning to apologize is learning to forgive. In fact, love really can't be called love if it does not include forgiveness. Forgiveness is recognizing a person's failures or offenses, but refusing to hold that person accountable for the pain he's inflicted on you. It releases; it does not punish. Forgiveness, though, is not for wimps. It is for the strong, the grounded, the secure, the truly loving—who are willing to graciously and gracefully pardon even a guilty party.

Understand that forgiveness is not a feeling; it is an act of your will.

Understand that forgiveness is not a feeling; it is an act of your will. It is a voluntary determination to release the person who has hurt you, even when your feelings are still tender or your heart is still broken. You must choose to forgive—sometimes moment by moment. But if you will keep choosing to forgive, the feelings will eventually follow.

Once you have forgiven, let the issue be finished. To finish it is to refuse to allow it to resurface occasionally and to refuse to let it influence your future feelings or behavior. Suffocate it; crucify it; decapitate it; and bury it. Don't you dare dig up the coffin of that painful issue when you want a good zinger to hurl at your man's heart. True forgiveness has a way of allowing two people who are in intimate relationship to *go on*. And going on, Leading Lady, is what your relationship is all about.

You're On

1. Are you good at apologizing when it's needed? What have you learned today that will help you more effectively communicate your remorse to the man in your life?

_____

_____

_____

_____

_____

_____

_____

_____

_____

_____

_____

_____

_____

_____

_____

> *Once you have forgiven, let the issue be finished. Suffocate it; crucify it; decapitate it; and bury it.*

2. Are you good at receiving apologies—or do you hold a grudge? How can you accept apologies more graciously and be more action focused as you respond when your man says, "I'm sorry"?

3. What people or situations do you claim to have forgiven, but know in your heart that you are not really "finished" with them? Will you finish them now?

_____

_____

_____

_____

_____

_____

_____

_____

_____

_____

_____

_____

_____

_____

Learn Your Lines

As far as the east is from the west,
so far has He removed our transgressions from us.
Psalm 103:12

For if you forgive men their trespasses, your heavenly Father
will also forgive you. But if you do not forgive men their
trespasses, neither will your Father forgive your trespasses.
Matthew 6:14, 15

Let all bitterness, wrath, anger, clamor and evil speaking
be put away from you, with all malice. And be kind to one
another, tenderhearted, forgiving one another,
even as God in Christ forgave you.
Ephesians 4:31, 32

COMING SOON

*I*f your relationship with your man has been a roller coaster of ups and downs, due to arguments, failures to apologize, withholding forgiveness, and allowing old offenses to still haunt you, aren't you looking forward to learning how to deal with disagreements more effectively? What good things do you think can come into your relationship with the man in your life now that you know how to deal with your disagreements and how to apologize, forgive, and finish a situation?

_____

_____

_____

_____

_____

_____

_____

_____

_____

_____

_____

_____

ACTION!

*B*ased on what you have learned in this chapter, what are three concise, measurable, attainable goals you will set for yourself as you learn to deal with conflict—from start to finish—more effectively? Be sure to include a schedule and target date for reaching each goal and a reward for accomplishing it.

1. Goal: _____

Schedule and target completion date: _____

Reward: _____

_____

2. Goal: _____

Schedule and target completion date: _____

Reward: _____

_____

3. Goal: _____

Schedule and target completion date: _____

Reward: _____

_____

Notes

Notes

11

The Lady's Needs and Wants

Introducing

he Bible says that "love will cover a multitude of sins" (1 Peter 4:8), but I need to tell you that love does not meet all of your needs. It is designed, of course, to bring fulfillment to some deep needs in your life, but there is not a relationship on earth in which both parties have all of their needs met by the other. When you are involved in a marriage or a relationship that is headed towards marriage, you need to know that your man was not created to fill every vacuum in your life. You'd be worn out in a hurry if you thought you had to meet all of his needs, wouldn't you? All right, so you can understand that he would be too.

At the same time, there are needs that the man in your life should and will meet. He is eager to please you, but he'll need some direction. For that reason, in the second part of this chapter, I want to help you learn to ask for what you want because your man is not likely to figure it out on his own. I think you'll see, though, that once you learn how to ask, you may be pleasantly surprised by his response.

The Main Event

Act 1: Don't Drain the Love Tank

Even in the post-women's liberation age and the "dispensation of equality" that we subscribe to, there still resides in the hearts and minds of some women—maybe not you, but some women—the idea that the man in a relationship is to be the strong one and the smart one, the provider and the protector, and that the woman is supposed to clean the house, iron his shirts, and say "yes" to his sexual advances. With that kind of collective thinking among women in the not-so-distant past, is it any wonder that the ladies are inclined to believe the lie that men are supposed to "take care of everything"?

In Chapter 2 of this workbook, we addressed the issue of fantasy, and I want to briefly touch on it again here. Perhaps you have dealt with fantasies about your man's becoming the next president of the United States or with the notion that a few more hours in the gym could give him the body of an Olympic athlete, but you are living in a fantasy world if you think any man is wonderful enough to be the only person you need in order for every aspect of your life to be fulfilled.

When a woman expects her man to meet all of her needs, she places a siphon on their love tank. She is also asking him to play God (Now that's an unrealistic expectation!), because God is the only one who can truly fulfill us and meet every need. Furthermore, when she is so focused on having

> *You are living in a fantasy world if you think any man is wonderful enough to be the only person you need in order for every aspect of your life to be fulfilled.*

her needs met, she fails to make deposits into the love reserve—and so you know what happens: it soon runs dry. But she is not to bear the responsibility of draining the tank alone, because you see, a man, with his performance orientation and his drive to be the best, will sometimes try to be the all-inclusive need meet-er. In fact, his ego goes pump-pump-pump when he realizes that you really *think* he is man enough to meet all the needs you have. Then, when he must face the God-ordained fact that he can't be that man, he feels like a failure. So you both need a healthy dose of reality.

Listed below are several areas of need that are common in a woman's life. Take a look at them, stop at each one, and ask yourself if you have placed an unhealthy or unrealistic expectation on your man to meet all of your needs in that particular area.

- Physical needs
- Emotional needs
- Intellectual needs
- Social needs
- Spiritual needs
- Needs for security
- Needs for achievement
- Needs for significance
- Needs for recreation and fun
- Needs for practical help
- Needs for "a little space"

> *When a woman expects her man to meet all of her needs, she places a siphon on their love tank.*

Now, look at the list again. This time, ask yourself how these needs can be fulfilled through other channels. For instance, you might have a friend who likes to walk or bicycle; get your recreational needs met by walking or riding bicycles with her (that'll help meet your social needs too). To satisfy your need for intellectual growth and challenge, get some books or join a discussion group. Of course, you yourself are the only person who can satisfy your need for personal space, so you have to be the one to do it.

You are a leading lady, and your life is large. There is enough of you to share with others without stealing from the man you love. Both of your lives, yours and his, will be enriched if you will relieve him of the pressure of the impossible task of having to meet all your needs. It's wonderful for him to be your "first and favorite;" just don't ask him to be your "one and only."

> *You are a leading lady, and your life is large. There is enough of you to share with others without stealing from the man you love.*

You're On

1. Have you been guilty of thinking your man can meet all of your needs—or wanting him to? What are some ways you have done that? What have been the results?

_____

_____

_____

_____

_____

_____

_____

_____

_____

_____

_____

_____

_____

_____

Your reasonable wishes are valid, and a man who loves you will be eager to accommodate you because, remember, he really does want to please you.

2. Realistically, what needs can your man meet and which ones can he not?

_____

_____

_____

_____

_____

_____

_____

_____

_____

_____

_____

*He is
eager to please
you, but he'll
need some
direction.*

_____

_____

_____

_____

_____

_____

_____

9. What are some of the needs you can meet on your own or through relationships with other people?

_____

_____

_____

_____

_____

_____

_____

_____

_____

_____

_____

_____

_____

_____

_____

_____

_____

_____

> **The fact that your man needs to be informed does not mean he doesn't love you, nor does it indicate that he is not "tuned in."**

Learn Your Lines

The Lord is my shepherd; I shall not want.
Psalm 23:1

*And my God shall supply all your needs according
to His riches in glory by Christ Jesus.*
Philippians 4:19

*Let us come boldly to the throne of grace, that we may
obtain mercy and find grace to help in time of need.*
Hebrews 4:16

Act 2: Ask for What You Want

I hope you now understand that you cannot expect your man to meet all of your needs; he simply cannot do it. But if the two of you are in an intimate relationship and in that context, certain needs should be met. For instance, if you are married, your sexual needs should be met in your relationship. In addition to your needs, though, you also have desires. Your reasonable wishes are valid, and a man who loves you will be eager to accommodate you, because remember, he really does want to please you.

Your man may have many terrific qualities and well-developed abilities, but I suspect that being a mind reader is not one of them. In fact, I can't recall ever meeting a woman who raved about her man's proficiency and intuitive capacity to know exactly what she wanted and when she wanted it.

Leading lady, your man cannot and will not know what you want unless you tell him. The fact that he needs to be informed does not mean he doesn't love you, nor does it indicate that he is not "tuned in." Don't make the mistake of assuming that, if he loves you, he should know what you want, or decide that if he doesn't know, he should ask. Maybe in your mind, he should ask, but let me tell you, he probably won't. This is just the way it is with men. They express love to you by giving and doing; they are not very good at asking or deducing.

You see, men tend to subscribe to a combination of two old adages: "If it ain't broke, don't fix it," and "The squeaky wheel gets the grease." In other words, if you don't speak up, he will assume nothing is wrong. When he believes everything is fine, he will not try to "fix" it. But rest assured, if the wheel squeaks (in other words, if you let him know what you want), you might see him spring into action and try to move heaven and earth to get an oil can. You may not always get what you want, but don't let it be because you didn't ask.

I encourage you right now to determine in your heart that you will not exploit his desires to please you, but that you will clearly and kindly communicate your desires.

Your man loves to feel needed, and he relishes opportunities to do for you. But he will feel taken advantage of if you constantly ask him to do things you can do for yourself or if your requests are unreasonable. I encourage you right now to determine in your heart that you will not exploit his desires to please you, but that you will clearly and kindly communicate your desires. From now on, before you ask him for something, first ask yourself the four questions below. If you answer "no," to any of them, ditch your request. If you answer "yes" to all of them, ask away!

- ◆ Is my request reasonable?
- ◆ Is my request realistic?
- ◆ Is my man the right person to ask?
- ◆ Is now the right time to ask him?

You're On

1. Have you been expecting your man to just "know" what you want and deliver? Do you now see that he really wants to please you, but that he'll need you to make specific requests?

_____

_____

2. How can you begin to clearly and kindly communicate your desires to your man?

_____

_____

_____

_____

_____

_____

3. If you are the quiet type, or if you feel guilty asking for what you want, what adjustments can you make in order to be more comfortable verbalizing your wishes?

_____

_____

_____

_____

_____

_____

_____

You may not always get what you want, but don't let it be because you didn't ask.

_____

_____

_____

_____

_____

_____

_____

_____

Learn Your Lines

*Ask and it will be given to you; seek, and you will find;
knock, and it will be opened to you. For everyone
who asks receives, and he who seeks finds,
and to him who knocks it will be opened.*

Matthew 7:7, 8

*Be anxious for nothing, but in everything by prayer
and supplication, with thanksgiving, let your requests
be made known to God.*

Philippians 4:6

Yet you do not have because you do not ask.

James 4:2b

COMING SOON

$\mathcal{L}$ife goes better when everybody's needs are being met, doesn't it? What are you looking forward to as you learn to have your needs met from a variety of sources and to tell your man what you want from him? What good things can come as the two of you learn to relate better, concerning your needs and desires?

_____

_____

_____

_____

_____

_____

_____

_____

_____

_____

_____

_____

_____

_____

_____

_____

ACTION!

*B*ased on what you have learned in this chapter, what are three concise, measurable, attainable goals you will set for yourself as you put into practice the lessons you've learned about getting your needs met and your wishes fulfilled? Be sure to include a schedule and target date for reaching each goal and a reward for accomplishing it.

1. Goal: _____

Schedule and target completion date: _____

Reward: _____

_____

2. Goal: _____

Schedule and target completion date: _____

Reward: _____

_____

3. Goal: _____

Schedule and target completion date: _____

Reward: _____

_____

Notes

Notes

12

The Lady Keeps the Love Alive

Introducing

Perhaps you are familiar with the Bible verse that says, "For everyone to whom much is given, from him much will be required" (Luke 12:48a). Leading lady, you are one to whom much is given. You are mightily gifted, and your life is abundantly blessed. I believe you will walk through the rest of your life with many opportunities to exhibit the greatness that is in you and that you will fulfill in grand style the destiny that God has for your life. I have encouraged you before in this workbook not to hide the gifts God has given you out of fear that you will lose the relationship that matters most to your heart and not to apologize for the ways He has blessed you. You've also learned not to leave your man in the audience or in the dressing room, to let him act out his love by contributing to your life. You know by now, too, the importance of giving him time to rehearse, communicating effectively, managing conflict, accepting him as he is, and allowing him to be transformed rather than trying to change him by your own efforts.

The time will come when the spotlight hits your life and your moment to take center stage will arrive. When it does, take him with you—and in the midst of it all, keep your love alive.

The Main Event

Act 1: Understand that Life Causes Leaks

The first step towards keeping your love alive through all the ups and downs, in and outs, and seemingly relentless demands of life is to refuse to let your love become routine. It should become more and more comfortable, but it should never become boring; it should never become "fine," and it should never become "good enough." One of the best ways to keep love alive and fresh is to be creative.

Oh, it isn't hard to be creative in the beginning of a relationship, especially before marriage when both parties are so eager to please. The man researches nice restaurants he can take his beloved to and asks his sister what he can do to really impress the woman of his dreams. She, on the other hand, learns to make Beef Wellington and covers the dinner table with rose petals when he comes over for a meal. Creativity isn't difficult in the midst of newlywed bliss, either. Enough said.

But as anniversaries and birthdays come and go, time and familiarity can poke tiny holes in a couple's love tank, and before you know it, love begins to leak. I write to you today about the itty-bitty, miniscule amounts of love that leak out every day. These leaks are not gushes; they are so small that they could not even be called drips or trickles. That's why they are so dangerous; you hardly notice them.

They are not caused by major crises; they are just the results of the ordinary stuff of life, but it's the ordinary stuff of life that causes people to lose their edge, especially people in love. The leaks are not dramatic, but we know they're there when people and activities that once delighted us simply are not fun anymore. That happens when meeting a deadline at work continually becomes more important than meeting your spouse for dinner. It happens when a woman slips out of her wife role in order to meet the demands of her role as a mother. It happens when the busy-ness of twenty-first century living subtly steals the joy of every day and the stress of our lives robs us of our ability to laugh. But, as you know, there will always be deadlines, there will always be children (or others with needs), there will always be busy-ness, and there will always be stress. Of everything I've listed, I am most certain that there will always be stress!

Amid life's challenges, your intimate relationship will not stay in neutral; either it will move forward and grow, or it will quietly and smoothly shift into reverse and deteriorate. If it shifts into reverse, the transition will occur so imperceptibly that you probably won't even know it has happened until you have traveled quite a distance down the road to trouble.

So what can you do in order to keep moving ahead? First of all, never consider times of happiness or ease to be opportunities to rest in your love. During the good times, keep expressing your love to your mate in new and different ways. Do something you've never done together. Realize that your relationship is growing, and find

> *As anniversaries and birthdays come and go, time and familiarity can poke tiny holes in a couple's love tank, and before you know it, love begins to leak.*

ways to anticipate, encourage, and accommodate even more growth. But more than that, commit to do more and to be more for the man in your life than you have done in the past—that is the essence of creativity.

Remember how you felt towards him when you first fell in love, and let those feelings show in your actions. In those early days, you tended to go "above and beyond the call of duty," didn't you? You gave him more casserole than he asked for; you changed the sheets more often; perhaps you even warmed his towels in the dryer. Those are the kinds of love expressions to which I urge your return. And in the next section of this chapter, I'll list some practical and creative ways for you to show your man that you are still as crazy about him as ever.

> *Never consider times of happiness or ease to be opportunities to rest in your love.*

You're On

1. Is your relationship with your man moving forward, or has it shifted into reverse?

_____

_____

_____

_____

_____

_____

_____

_____

2. How do the challenges and pressures of everyday living affect your relationship with the man you love?

_____

_____

_____

_____

_____

_____

_____

_____

_____

_____

_____

_____

_____

_____

_____

_____

_____

Commit to do more and to be more for the man in your life than you have done in the past—that is the essence of creativity.

3. How can you begin to regain the freshness and the edge of your earlier intimate relationship?

I urge you to return to the love expressions of the early days of your relationship with your man.

Learn Your Lines

If the ax is dull, and one does not sharpen the edge,
then he must use more strength; but wisdom brings success.
Ecclesiastes 10:10

For everyone to whom much is given,
from him much will be required.
Luke 12:48a

And this I pray, that your love may abound still
more and more in knowledge and all discernment.
Philippians 1:9

But as for you, brethren, do not grow weary in doing good.
2 Thessalonians 3:13

Act 2: Practical Ways to Keep Your Love Alive

◆ Warm his towel in the dryer.

◆ Find some old pictures of the two of you, photos taken when the light of new love was dancing in your eyes. Frame them and display them throughout your home.

◆ Keep verbalizing why you love him.

◆ Touch him unexpectedly.

◆ Cook dinner for him—not the way you do now, the way you *used* to.

◆ Splurge on some bath products and take a long, leisurely bath together.

◆ Write a love note on his bathroom mirror—in lipstick.

◆ Sprinkle a trail of rose petals from the place he parks his car all the way to the bedroom.

◆ Pray for him and with him.

◆ Laugh as often as possible. Do your best to inspire and encourage joy.

◆ You've already read this, but I can't say it enough: shower him with praise and affirmation.

◆ Clear off the clutter from your bedside tables and replace it with candles. Light them at bedtime.

◆ Say good things about him in front of other people.

◆ Give your man a wallet-sized wedding picture of the two of you—even if the wedding was years ago.

◆ Don't "let yourself go." Keep your skin, hair and nails in good condition. Stay in shape physically. Pay attention to your clothes and learn to apply your make-up like a pro.

◆ Tell him all the ways you believe in him; be specific.

◆ Arrange an outing for your man and his buddies. Get tickets to a sporting event, a car show, or whatever they enjoy.

◆ Have a nice photo taken of yourself, frame it, and give it to him.

◆ Tell him how much you missed him when he comes home from work.

◆ Watch a ballgame with him—and sit as close as you can get.

◆ Have his car detailed.

◆ Get sexy new lingerie, and wear it.

◆ Value certain things just because they are important to your man.

◆ Make a grown-up brag book. Document everything you love about him.

◆ Tell him how thankful you are for him, and be specific.

You're On

1. In the course of your relationship with the man you love, what is the most creative expression of love you have ever offered him? How did he respond?

_____

_____

_____

_____

_____

_____

_____

_____

_____

_____

_____

_____

_____

_____

_____

_____

_____

_____

2. Which of the ideas listed do you think would be most meaningful to the man in your life?

_____

_____

_____

_____

_____

_____

_____

_____

_____

_____

_____

_____

_____

_____

_____

_____

Laugh as often as possible. Do your best to inspire and encourage joy.

3. What other creative ideas can you think of to help keep your love alive?

_____

_____

_____

_____

_____

_____

_____

_____

_____

Pray with him and for him.

_____

_____

_____

_____

_____

_____

_____

_____

_____

Learn Your Lines

An excellent wife is the crown of her husband . . .
Proverbs 12:4

And above all things have fervent love for one another,
for "love will cover a multitude of sins."
1 Peter 4:8

My little children, let us not love in word or in tongue,
but in deed and in truth.
1 John 3:18

COMING SOON

*W*hat are your thoughts, hopes, and dreams as you look forward to keeping your love alive? How are you going to guard against love leaks in your life with your man? How are you going to implement some of the creative ideas you have learned in this chapter and come up with some of your own?

ACTION!

$\mathcal{B}$ased on what you have learned in this chapter, what are three concise, measurable, attainable goals you will set for yourself as you learn to keep alive the most important human relationship in your life? Be sure to include a schedule and target date for reaching each goal and a reward for accomplishing it.

1. Goal: _____

Schedule and target completion date: _____

Reward: _____

_____

2. Goal: _____

Schedule and target completion date: _____

Reward: _____

_____

3. Goal: _____

Schedule and target completion date: _____

Reward: _____

_____

Notes

Appendix A: Goals at a Glance

Take a few moments to review the goals you set for yourself in the "Action!" sections at the end of each chapter. Compile them on the lines below. Keep them grouped the way they are in the workbook, using one blank for each goal. For example, list each of your three goals from Chapter 1 on the blanks next to number 1—using one blank for each goal. Then for every chapter's goals put a star or a circle around the one that is most important to you. This will help you set your priorities. You might want to consider keeping that short list of most important goals in your appointment book, on your daily calendar, or on your refrigerator.

Chapter 1   1. _____   2. _____   3. _____

Chapter 2   1. _____   2. _____   3. _____

Chapter 3   1. _____   2. _____   3. _____

Chapter 4   1. _____   2. _____   3. _____

Chapter 5   1. _____   2. _____   3. _____

Chapter 6   1. _____   2. _____   3. _____

Chapter 7   1. _____   2. _____   3. _____

Chapter 8   1. _____   2. _____   3. _____

Chapter 9   1. _____   2. _____   3. _____

Chapter 10   1. _____   2. _____   3. _____

Chapter 11   1. _____   2. _____   3. _____

Chapter 12   1. _____   2. _____   3. _____

Appendix B: Message to a Leading Lady

Leading lady, I do not know the full scope of your experiences with men, but I'd like to share some things with you. Perhaps other men cannot or will not articulate these things to you, so if you will, let me represent them, for because I am a man, they are my brothers.

On behalf of every man who has ever been the reason for a tear on your pillow, on behalf of every man who has ever caused you pain or made you feel as though you climbed the ladder of success alone, I'm sorry. I am truly, truly sorry.

On behalf of every man that you have prayed for and encouraged and supported and comforted and blessed by your presence; on behalf of every man whose power you have pointed out; on behalf of every man with whom you have been patient, thank you. From the bottom of my heart, thank you.

And on behalf of every man to whom you'll go home — or the one you'll someday go home — I say, "Give me time. Let's rehearse it. Let's get it right. Let's stand together on center stage, loving God and loving each other. Let me be God's leading man with God's leading lady!"

Appendix C: Dealing with Other Men in Your Life

There are only two sexes that populate planet earth, so your relationship with that special man in your life is not the only relationship you will have with a man. You may have had a relationship with your father, or a father figure, for years, and you may leave the presence of the man you love every morning to join other men at your workplace. So, I'd like to offer you some helpful advice on dealing with the host of other men who surround you.

Your Father or Father Figure

Ever since you were born, you may have been Daddy's Little Girl. A strong, healthy relationship with your father can do wonders to help prepare you for a relationship with the man you will eventually marry, but when you enter into that committed, lasting relationship, you are no longer a little girl and you no longer belong to Daddy as you once did.

Where your relationship with your man will require many adjustments, your relationship with your father may be as comfortable as an easy chair. Where your relationship with your man includes both the wonder and the curiosities of newness, your relationship with your father is established. And so, you may feel safer at times with your dad, but it is time for the man in your life to take first place.

Both you and your father will have to allow this good and proper transition to occur. You may have to be more assertive in the process than you are comfortable with, but let me tell you how to recognize when it's time for Daddy to move over.

◆ If you see that your father and your man have gotten into competition, speak up and ask Dad to move over.

◆ If your father is "meddling" in your life (especially your love life), if he is still attempting to make decisions for you or to direct things for you, speak up and ask Dad to move over.

◆ If you frequently make statements to your man that begin with, "Well, my daddy . . ." In this case, your man is the one who will let you know what *frequently* means. In this case, don't speak up, shut up.

◆ If you begin to think of your man as "less" than your father or deem his opinions or decisions not as good as your father's, stop. He is not your father, and his approach to life may not match your father's. He is, however, the man you chose, so adjust your attitude and treat him with respect.

In the end, having your father in an appropriate role can be a blessing to both you and your man. Having him involved in your life inappropriately can be a curse and cause misery for all of you. So be strong, put top priority on your relationship with your man, assure your dad of your long-term affection for him, and love both of them in healthy, appropriate ways.

The Men at Work

There are so many different ways in which you can interact with the men at your workplace. You may have a male boss, or you may have men who report to you as their boss. You may be part of a team or work group with men, or you may work with men whose jobs place them on the same level with you.

◆ When corresponding with men in an e-mail, keep it very short and to the point. Men want to roll their eyes when they open an e-mail that is filled with long paragraphs and lengthy explanations.

◆ In your verbal and written communication, rely on verbs more than nouns. In addition, you can usually leave out many of the adjectives you might like to use.

◆ In your written correspondence, use bullet points instead of sentences whenever possible.

◆ Do not go out alone to a meal or a social event with a male colleague. Ask someone else to join you. If at all possible, do not ride in a car alone with a male who is not your husband or your boyfriend. (Men at work usually make complicated boyfriends anyway!)

◆ When you are the boss and men report to you, treat them as you do all of your employees: with dignity and respect. Especially when they are younger (or act younger) than you, resist the temptation to mother them. Be careful, too, with requests that you want to make of a male employee "because he's a guy."

◆ When your boss is a man, treat him with professionalism and respect. Especially if you are fairly new to the workforce or have unresolved issues with your dad, do not regard your boss as a substitute for your father.

◆ When you are married or involved in a committed relationship, be very clear about the fact that you are happily unavailable. One way to do this is to prominently display a picture of yourself and the man you love.

◆ If you are not married, think twice before getting involved in an office romance. Talk about a potentially sticky situation!

◆ Set your standards and keep them.

Notes

Notes

Notes

Notes

Notes

Notes

Notes

BISHOP *T. D. JAKES*
INVITES YOU TO TAKE YOUR PLACE ON LIFE'S CENTER STAGE WITH

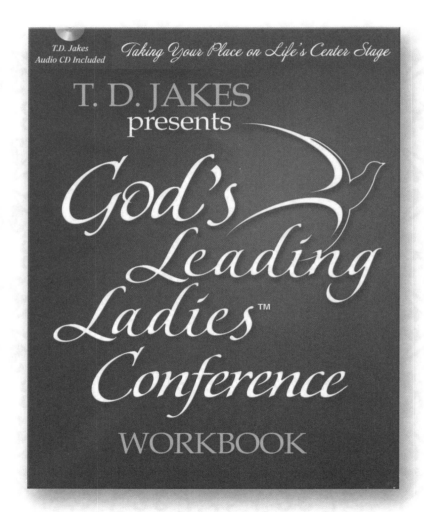

Available now at God's Leading Ladies Conferences, www.thomasnelson.com, and your favorite Christian retailer.